Advance Praise for
Millionaire Teacher: The Nine Rules of
Wealth You Should Have Learned in School

Andrew Hallam's book is just the right one for novice investors. He not only provides the winning strategy in terms of your personal financial life, but in investing as well. The book contains Hallam's Nine Rules to become a millionaire, and he has them all right. If you know people who are financial train wrecks waiting to happen, recommend this book to them. It may be the best investment they make.

Larry Swedroe
Author, *The Quest for Alpha*, Principal and Director of Research, The Buckingham Family of Financial Services

Millionaire Teacher is an enormously thoughtful gem of an investment book that every serious investor should read, study, and learn from. This wise and witty book gives the reader a fresh perspective on the simple concepts needed to sustain financial freedom. Most of all, it is delivered with a genuine simplicity that will capture the reader's attention from the first page and hold it to the end.

Bill Schultheis
Author, *The New CoffeeHouse Investor*, Principal of Soundmark Wealth Management, LLC

Every once in a great while I read a financial book that I think should be shared with everyone I know. *Millionaire Teacher* is that book!

Charles E. Kirk, *The Kirk Report*

Unlike most investment book authors, Andrew Hallam has become a millionaire by living frugally and investing HIS OWN MONEY successfully. His book is a great guide for the average person seeking financial independence.

Michael B. O'Higgins
O'Higgins Asset Management, Inc.,
Author, *Beating the Dow, Beating the Dow with Bonds*

Andrew Hallam is proof that you don't need a high salary, complex stock trading system or even a financial adviser to achieve financial independence. You can get rich by living within your means and using simple wealth-building tools such as low-cost index funds. *Millionaire Teacher* is a sensible and highly readable guide to investing that packs a lot of wisdom into its nine simple rules. There are important lessons here for everyone, from newbie investors to experienced stock pickers.

John Heinzl, Business/Finance columnist, *The Globe and Mail*

Andrew's book is my "go to" book from here on out when asked for a recommendation for that graduating high school or college student. It is a joy to read and will undoubtedly raise the financial literacy of young people as well as adults.

Robert Wasilewski, President RW Investment Strategies
Author, *Do-It Yourself (DIY) Investor* blog

Millionaire Teacher

The Nine Rules of Wealth You
Should Have Learned in School

Millionaire Teacher

The Nine Rules of Wealth You
Should Have Learned in School

ANDREW HALLAM

WILEY
John Wiley & Sons (Asia) Pte Ltd

Other Wiley Editorial Offices

John Wiley & Sons, 111 River Street, Hoboken, NJ 07030, USA

John Wiley & Sons, The Atrium, Southern Gate, Chichester, West Sussex, P019 8SQ, United
Kingdom

John Wiley & Sons (Canada) Ltd., 5353 Dundas Street West, Suite 400, Toronto, Ontario, M9B
6HB, Canada

John Wiley & Sons Australia Ltd., 42 McDougall Street, Milton, Queensland 4064,
Australia

Wiley-VCH, Boschstrasse 12, D-69469 Weinheim, Germany

Library of Congress Cataloging-in-Publication Data

ISBN: 978-0-470-83006-2 (Paperback)
ISBN: 978-0-470-83008-6 (ePDF)
ISBN: 978-0-470-83007-9 (eMobi)
ISBN: 978-0-470-82819-9 (ePub)

Typeset in 10.5/11.5pt ITC Garamond by MPS Limited, a Macmillan Company, Chennai

10 9 8 7 6 5 4 3 2

*To my mom and dad (Roger and Hilary Hallam)
for your love, guidance, and model of what
a fabulous marriage is meant to be.*

And to Pele Hallam-Young, for being such an amazing wife.

Contents

Acknowledgments

I'd like to thank Ian McGugan, for encouraging me to write this book, and for showing me what great financial writing is supposed to look like. To the teachers at Singapore American School, who prompted me to write an understandable guide for the layperson. Many of you have turned an important corner by saying no to the excessive fees charged by certain financial service operators, and I'm excessively proud of you for that.

Hats off to Kris Olson, Keith Wakelin, Deb Wakelin, Neerav Bhatt, Gordon Cyr, and Seng Su Lin for allowing me to pry into their financially empowered personal lives for the betterment of others.

And for helping a technological Luddite, cheers to Excel master, Dan Skimin; the Jedi of patience, Lavinia Vasundran; technological coach, Dianna Pratt; and graphics guru, Paul Welsh.

Thank you to Facebook master Alex Wong; webmaster of infinite degrees, David Dixon; artist supreme, Fang Yang; my secret agent, John Kimzey; and the supplier of nutritional power, Jane Antique.

Nick Wallwork, of John Wiley & Sons, deserves my sincere gratitude for believing in this project, as do production master, Janis Soo; editor extraordinaire, Jennifer Wells, and the marketing tag team of Cynthia Mak and Cindy Chu.

Finally, thanks to my wife, Pele Hallam-Young, for her unwavering encouragement. Every day with her is Christmas.

Foreword

Every magazine editor cringes when a plain brown envelope with an unsolicited manuscript arrives in the mail. Chances are, it contains a letter that begins: "Dear fellow truth seeker. The international conspiracy to control our minds with fluoride is revealed in the 15,000-word article enclosed. Call me immediately to discuss when you will be publishing it."

Despite the cranks, an editor lives in the hope that one of those plain brown envelopes may lead to something great. I can tell you that once a decade or so, that hope actually materializes. My proof? Andrew Hallam.

I had never met Andrew when an envelope landed on my desk at *MoneySense* magazine <www.moneysense.ca/>. It contained a typewritten article about Warren Buffett. I remember reading the piece in my office and staring out over Front Street in Toronto as I debated what to do. The writer's enthusiasm jumped off the page; he also seemed unusually knowledgeable. On the other hand, who was the writer, this Andrew Hallam guy? And why did he spell Buffett's name with just one *t*?

I decided to phone Andrew and I will always be glad that I did. He explained to me that he was a teacher on Vancouver Island. Investing was his passion. And, sure, he would be happy to rework his piece a bit and even give Mr. Buffett his full consignment of *t*'s.

The article turned out well, and over the next few years, Andrew became a regular contributor to our pages. He filed fascinating stories on the stock market, the art of haggling, and, eventually, on his decision to move to Singapore and take up a teaching job there at a school for international students.

Somewhere along the way, it became clear to me that Andrew was living, breathing proof that all the theory about personal finance could actually work in practice. He was a middle-income earner, and someone with no ties to Wall Street. But it was clear from his stories that he was amassing wealth at impressive speed.

Exactly how he was accomplishing so much was still unclear to me. Andrew and I always communicated by phone or e-mail, so I could only guess what he was like in person. That all changed when he arranged an opportunity for me to come to Singapore and teach a weeklong session on writing to his students at the Singapore American School.

Meeting Andrew face-to-face for the first time, I was struck by three things. First (and I realize how superficial this sounds) I couldn't help but notice that Andrew was seriously buff.

Unlike those of us who come from the keg-shaped end of the physical spectrum, Andrew is one of those annoying, long-muscled ectomorphs who look as if they were designed to lope endlessly across wide savannas. He had told me he was a distance runner; I hadn't realized he was good enough to win races against thousands of competitors. Every day in the week to come, I would see Andrew pull on a pair of running shoes and speed off to run distances that would have had me hailing a taxi and packing a lunch. He monitored his training with stopwatch precision.

The second characteristic I noticed about Andrew was his good cheer. That week, and in years to come, I would see Andrew face stress. I have never, though, seen him downcast or angry or petty.

The final thing about Andrew that caught my attention is his joy in teaching. Watching him bring a class of 15-year-olds to attention, then prompt, prod, and delight them through a lesson, made me realize that high school teachers are not given nearly enough credit for the miracles they accomplish every day.

So what does all this have to do with money? In this book, Andrew will tell you about his own experiences on the road to prosperity. But if I could underline one small portion of what he so ably communicates, it's the importance of seeing money as part of a much broader experience.

Andrew has managed to accumulate wealth while also being a competitive athlete and an involved teacher, not to mention a happy, contented individual. His book demonstrates that you don't have to be a tax accountant or a scrooge to wind up rich.

He approaches the topic of wealth building with an outlook that owes a great deal to his background in distance running. His recommended regimen begins with realism. Champions can't lie their way to victory. They have to accept that training for a race involves a sustained effort over time.

The same goes with personal finance. Unlike many authors, Andrew isn't here to sell you a get-rich-quick scheme. What he will do, though, is show you how a simple program followed over the years can help you build wealth faster than nearly all your neighbors. In fact, he explains how you can do better than 80 percent of investors simply by avoiding the high-priced products that financial advisers try to stuff into your portfolio.

Some writers attempt to scare you with predictions of financial apocalypse. Others try to thrill you with promises of the huge profits to be made in some hot sector. Andrew avoids both schools of silliness. Instead, with his usual good cheer, he shows you how a habit of optimism about the broad economy pays off in the long run—even in the middle of financial crisis. Especially if you're a young investor, you will be fascinated to learn that you should be praying for the market to fall, not rise.

Andrew delivers his message in a way that anyone can appreciate. His writing is funny, personal, upbeat—and a withering critique of the many ways that the financial industry sabotages our attempts to build wealth. As you might expect from a gifted teacher, he manages to be both rigorous and accessible.

Andrew's book is a joyous but realistic guide to how middle-income earners can amass the wealth they deserve. I'm glad I opened that brown envelope many years ago; you'll be equally glad that you opened the pages of this book.

Ian McGugan

Ian McGugan is the features editor at *The Globe and Mail* and the founding editor of *MoneySense* magazine.

Introduction

If you were considering a profession and you wanted to become wealthy, certain lines of traditionally high-paying work might tempt you. Would it be law, medicine, business, or dentistry? Few, if any, would choose my profession if they aspired to be rich. I'm a high school English teacher—a middle-class professional if there ever was one. Yet I became a debt-free millionaire in my 30s.

I didn't take exceptional risks with my money and I didn't inherit a penny from anyone. When I went to college, I paid the entire bill myself. How did I pay for my own schooling and amass more than a million debt-free dollars before my fortieth birthday? Fortunately, I learned from (and was inspired by) some financially savvy characters, who urged me to master what I should have learned in high school. Because financial literacy isn't adequately taught in most high schools, you might be among the millions who were shortchanged by our education system. This book is my attempt to make it up to you.

As a high school student, did you ever sit in an algebra class, an English class, a history or biology class and wonder: "What kind of real-world benefit is this going to have on my life? Are Hamlet's soliloquies, the formulas in trigonometry, or the intimate knowledge of a dead piglet's inner workings really going to benefit me outside the walls of the classroom?" There is no easy answer to these questions.

But the subject of money is undeniably essential. Unlike a pig dissection or a challenging algebraic formula, everyone benefits by mastering it. Most families don't want to talk about money around the house though. It gets as much conversational airtime as the extended family oddball that nobody admits being related to anymore. You know—the promising uncle and his mail-order bride who both work as directors in the exotic film industry.

Want proof that money is a taboo subject? Did your parents share how long it took them to pay off their house, and what factors affected this? Did they explain how credit cards worked, and where and how they invested their money? Did they provide insight into how they chose your family's cars over the years? Did they reveal how they paid for those cars, or what kinds of taxes they owed on their homes and incomes? In most cases, they probably didn't.

Without a sound financial education, students can graduate from top universities with starry academic titles, but with little more financial knowledge than an eighth grader. Once they enter the workforce, they might as well be walking outside naked during a winter's blizzard.

But don't blame your parents, high school teachers, or college professors for your frostbitten butt. Most of them stumbled into their own snowstorm, years ago, grabbing the odd garment as they raced out the door of their homes.

Poor planning and inadequate financial educations cause too many people to fall into poor consumption habits and weak investments, especially when trying to keep up with the profligate spending habits of their neighbors, the Jones, who seem to have it all.

You can't follow Mr. Jones's habits if you want to grow rich. You can't spend like him. You can't borrow like him. And you certainly can't invest like him.

Mr. Jones, after all, invests money with the average financial adviser who promises wealth, or at the very least, an eventual, sound retirement. But too many advisers are like the character of the wealthy Pardoner in Geoffrey Chaucer's *Canterbury Tales*, with one important difference: When the Pardoner extorted money from Christian pilgrims—with the promise of a heavenly reward—the payoff was in plain view (unlike today's hidden advisory fees). The majority of financial planners don't have interests that are aligned with yours, no matter how friendly they appear. Because you didn't learn this in school, you'll likely find yourself with the wrong investment products and paying hidden fees toward someone else's Mercedes-Benz. This book will help you avoid that pitfall.

But why should you bother with my book when hundreds of others distill similar themes? To explain that, I need to tell you why I wrote *Millionaire Teacher*.

Many of my teaching colleagues became aware that—besides teaching English—I had also published numerous articles on personal finance, two of which were nominated as finalists for National Publishing Awards for financial writing in Canada.

For that reason, they asked me to teach them about money. I wanted, however, to deliver more than a handful of seminars. I wanted to find the simplest books I could on the concept of sound investing, buy boxes full of them, and gift them to my colleagues.

So I did just that, buying 80 books that represented 12 different titles. Then, as if I were teaching a group of English students, I met the readers in small groups to discuss what they had learned.

But there was a problem. Many of the terms used by the financial authors were as decipherable as Egyptian hieroglyphics to my colleagues. Too many financial writers don't seem to realize much of what they write flies over the head of the average person.

I needed a different vehicle to extend my teaching, so I created this book with help from more than 100 of my friends and colleagues. Continuing to hold free financial seminars, I probably did more questioning than lecturing to find out what the average university-educated person understood about money so I could teach to the broadest possible audience.

When writing *Millionaire Teacher,* I shared my work with dozens of non-financially minded people who were keen to learn about investing. They provided feedback about what they understood and what they didn't, so I could make necessary changes to either explain financial jargon or avoid using it.

The result is this book: written by a millionaire teacher who listened closely to his students. In it, I share the nine rules of wealth you should have learned in school . . . but didn't. You will learn how to spend like a millionaire and invest with the very best, while avoiding the trappings of fear, greed, and the manipulations of those wanting their hands on your wallet. I followed these timeless, easy-to-apply rules and became a debt-free millionaire in my 30s. Now let me pass them on to you.

Note: All online links are operational at the time of writing.

Spend Like You Want to Grow Rich

I wasn't rich as a 30-year-old. Yet if I wanted to, I could have leased a Porsche, borrowed loads of money for an expensive, flashy home, and taken five-star holidays around the world. I would have looked rich, but instead, I would have been living on an umbilical cord of bank loans and credit cards. Things aren't always what they appear to be.

In 2004, I was tutoring an American boy in Singapore. His mom dropped him off at my house every Saturday. She drove the latest Jaguar, which in Singapore would have cost well over $250,000 (cars in Singapore are very expensive). They lived in a huge house, and she wore an elegant Rolex watch. I thought they were rich.

After a series of tutoring sessions the woman gave me a check. Smiling, she gushed about her family's latest overseas holiday, and expressed how happy she was that I was helping her son.

The check she wrote was for $150. Climbing on my bicycle after she left, I pedaled down the street and deposited the check in the bank.

But here's the thing: The check bounced—she didn't have enough money in her account. This could, of course, happen to anyone. With this family, however, it happened with as much regularity as a Kathmandu power outage. Dreading the phone calls where she would implore me to wait a week before cashing the latest check finally took its toll, and I eventually told her that I wouldn't be able to tutor her son anymore.

Was this supposed to be happening? After all, this woman had to be rich. She drove a Jaguar. She lived in a massive house. She wore a Rolex. Her husband was an investment banker who should have been doing the backstroke in the pools of money he made.

It dawned on me that she might not have been rich at all. Just because someone collects a large paycheck and lives like Persian royalty doesn't necessarily mean he or she is rich.

The Hippocratic Rule of Wealth

If we're interested in building wealth, perhaps we should all make a pledge to ourselves much like a doctor's Hippocratic oath: above all, DO NO HARM. We're living in an era of instant gratification. If we want to communicate with someone half a world away, we can do that immediately with a text message or a phone call. If we want to purchase something and have it delivered to our door, it's possible to do that with a mobile phone and a credit-card number—even if we don't have the money to pay for it.

Just like that seemingly wealthy American family in Singapore, it's very easy to harm our financial future by blowing money we don't even have. The story of living beyond one's means can be heard around the world.

To stay out of harm's way financially, we need to build assets, not debts. One of the surest ways to build wealth over a lifetime is to spend far less than you make and intelligently invest the difference. But too many people hurt their financial health by failing to differentiate between their "wants" and their "needs."

Many of us know people who landed great jobs right out of college and started down a path of hyperconsumption. It usually began innocently. Perhaps, with their handy credit cards they bought a new dining room table, but then their plates and cutlery didn't match so they had to upgrade.

Then there's the couch, which now doesn't jive with the fine dining room table. Thank God for Visa—time for a sofa upgrade. It doesn't take long, however, before our friends notice the carpet doesn't match the new couch, so they scour advertisements for a deal on a Persian beauty. Next, they're dreaming about a new entertainment system, then a home renovation, followed by the well-deserved trip to Hawaii.

Rather than living the American Dream, they're stuck in a mythological Greek nightmare. Zeus punished Sisyphus by forcing him to continually roll a boulder up a mountain, only to have it maddeningly roll back every time it neared the summit. Many consumers face the same relentless treadmill with their consumption habits. When they get close to paying off their debts, they reward themselves by adding weight to their Sisyphean stone, which knocks them back to the base of their own daunting mountain.

Buying something after saving for it (instead of buying it with a credit card) is so 1950s—at least, that's how many consumers see it. As a result, the twenty-first century has brought mountains of personal debt that often gets pushed under the rug.

Before we learn to invest to build wealth, we have to learn how to save. If we want to grow rich on a middle-class salary, we can't be average. We have to sidestep the consumption habits to which so many others have fallen victim.

According to *The Wall Street Journal*, the average U.S. household in 2010 was strapped with $7,490 in credit-card debt.[1] A *Huffington Post* business article reported in 2011 that 23 percent of Americans owed more money on their mortgages than their homes were actually worth. In Nevada, 66 percent of homeowners could sell their houses and still not have enough money to pay off their mortgages.[2]

Now here's where things get interesting. You might assume it's mostly low-salaried workers who overextend themselves. But consider this:

According to U.S. author and wealth researcher, Thomas Stanley, who has been surveying America's affluent since 1973, most U.S. homes valued at a million dollars or more (as of 2009) were not owned by millionaires. Instead, the majority of million-dollar homes were owned by nonmillionaires with large mortgages and very expensive tastes.[3] In sharp contrast, 90 percent of those who met the defined criterion to be a millionaire—having a net worth of more than $1 million—lived in homes valued at less than a million dollars.[4]

If there were such a thing as a financial Hippocratic oath, many people would be committing malpractice on themselves. It's fine to spend extravagantly if you're truly wealthy. But regardless of how high people's salaries are, if they can't live well without their job, then they aren't truly rich.

How would I define wealth?

It's important to make the distinction between real wealth and a wealthy pretense so that you don't get sucked into a lifestyle led by the wealthy pretenders of the world. Wealth itself is always relative. But for people to be considered wealthy, they should meet the following two criteria:

1. They should have enough money to never have to work again, if that's their choice.

2. They should have investments, a pension, or a trust fund that can provide them with twice the level of their country's median household income over a lifetime.

According to the U.S. Census Bureau, the median U.S. household income in 2009 was $50,221.[5] Based on my definition of wealth, if an American's investments can annually generate twice that amount ($100,442 or more), then that person is rich.

Earning twice as much money as the median household in your home country—without having to work—is a financial luxury many people can only dream about.

How do investments generate enough cash?

Because this book will focus on building investments using the stock and bond markets, let's use a relative example. If John builds an investment portfolio of $2.5 million, then he could feasibly sell four percent of that portfolio each year, equating to roughly $100,000 annually, and never run out of money. If his investments are able to continue growing by six to seven percent a year, he could likely afford, over time, to sell slightly more of his investment portfolio each year to cover the rising costs of living.

If John were in this position, I would consider him wealthy. If he also owned a Ferrari and a million-dollar home, then I'd consider him extremely wealthy.

But if John had an investment portfolio of $400,000, owned a million-dollar home with the help of a large mortgage, and leased a Ferrari, then I would suggest that John wasn't rich at all, even if his take-home pay was $600,000 a year.

I'm not suggesting that we live like misers and save every penny we earn. I've tried that already (as I'll share with you) and it's not much fun. But if we want to grow rich we need to have a purposeful plan, and watching what we spend so we can invest money is an important first step. If wealth building were a course that everyone took and if we were graded on it every year (even after high school), do you know who would fail the course miserably? Professional basketball players.

Most National Basketball Association (NBA) players make millions of dollars a year, but are they rich? Most of them seem to be. But it's not how much money you make that counts: it's what you do with what you make. According to a 2008 *Toronto Star* article, a NBA Players' Association representative visiting the Toronto Raptors team once warned the players to temper their spending by reminding them that 60 percent of retired NBA players go broke five years after they stop collecting their enormous NBA paychecks.[6] How can that happen? Sadly, the average NBA basketball player has very little (if any) financial common sense. Why would he? High schools don't prepare us for the financial world.

By following the concepts of wealth in this book, you can work your way toward financial independence. With a strong commitment to the rules, you could even grow wealthy—truly wealthy. This starts by following the first of my nine wealth rules: spend like you want to be rich. By minimizing the purchases that you don't really need, you can maximize your money for investment purposes.

Of course, that's often easier said than done when you see so many others purchasing things that you would like to have as well. Instead of looking where you think the grass is greener, admire your own yard, and compare it, if you must, to my father's old car. Doing so can build a foundation of wealth. Let me explain how it worked for me.

Can You See the Road When You're Driving?

Riding shotgun as a 15-year-old in my dad's 1975 Datsun, I thought we were traveling a bit fast. I leaned over to look at the speedometer and noticed that it didn't work. "Dad," I asked, "how do you know how fast you're going if your speedometer doesn't work?"

My dad asked me to lift up the floor mat beneath my feet. "Fold it back," he grinned. There was a fist-sized hole in the floor beneath my feet, and I could see the rushing road below. "Who needs a speedometer when you can get a better feel for speed by looking at the road," he told me.

The following year when I turned 16, I bought my own car with cash that I had saved from working at a supermarket. It was a six-year-old, 1980 Honda Civic. The speedometer worked, and best of all, there wasn't a draft at my feet. Because it was the nicest car in the family, I always felt like I was riding in style, which leads me to one of the greatest secrets of wealth building: your perceptions dictate your spending habits.

The surest way to grow rich over time is to start by spending a lot less than you make. If you can alter your perspective to be satisfied with what you have, then you won't be as tempted to blow your earnings. You'll be able to invest money over long periods of time, and thanks to the compounding miracles of the stock market, even middle-class wage earners eventually can amass sizable investment accounts. Thanks to my dad's car (which also leaked), I felt rich because I had a roadworthy steed that didn't leak from the roof and windows when it rained. Instead of comparing my car with those that were newer, faster, and cooler, I viewed my dad's car (which you could start with a screwdriver in the ignition slot) as the comparative benchmark.

Buddhists believe that "wanting" leads to suffering. In the case of the boy I tutored in Singapore, the family's seemingly insatiable appetite for fine things will likely lead to a degree of suffering—especially if the head of the family loses his job or wants to retire. It reminds me of a bumper sticker I once saw, parodying the infamous line of Snow White's dwarves: "I owe, I owe, it's off to work I go."

Why the aspiring rich should drive rich people's cars

If you want to give yourselves decent odds at growing rich, you don't have to drive a piece of junk. Where's the fun in that? How about driving the sort of car driven by the average U.S. millionaire? At first it might sound counterproductive to dole out many tens of thousands of dollars for a BMW, Mercedes-Benz, or Ferrari while expecting to grow rich. But most millionaires might surprise you with their taste in cars. In 2009, the median price paid for a car by U.S. millionaires was US$31,367.[7] Forget about expensive European darlings such as BMW, Mercedes-Benz, and Jaguar, as the favorite steeds of the rich. When Thomas Stanley polled U.S. millionaires, the most popular brand of car was the humdrum Toyota.[8]

Many of the wannabe rich try to outdo their peers in the car-spending department, easily parting with $40,000 and upward on a luxury cruiser, compared with the $31,367 the average U.S. millionaire pays. But how can you build wealth and reduce financial stress when you're paying far more for a car than an average millionaire? It's like trying to keep up with a pack of Olympic sprinters, but giving them a 50-meter head start.

Image is nothing if you lose your job, can't make your car payments, or if you're stuck having to work until you're 80 years old.

If you want to keep pace with the millionaires, begin on the start line or give yourself the biggest lead you can. It doesn't make sense to spend more than most rich people do on a set of wheels.

Paying more for a car than a decamillionaire

In 2006, Warren Buffett, one of the three richest men in the world bought the most expensive car he has ever owned: a $55,000 Cadillac.[9] The average decamillionaire—a person with a net worth of more than $10 million—paid $41,997 for his or her latest car.[10] If you find yourself at an upscale mall, check out the parking lot and you'll see many vehicles worth more than

$41,997. Some will even be worth more than Warren Buffett's car. But how many of the car owners do you think have $10 million or more? If your answer is "probably none" then you're catching on fast. Many have jeopardized their own pursuit of wealth or financial independence for the allusion of looking wealthy instead of being wealthy.

Whatever money you save on a car (not to mention the savings from interest payments if you can't buy the car outright) can go toward wealth-building investments.

Cars aren't investments. Unlike long-term assets such as real estate, stocks, and bonds, cars depreciate in value with each passing year.

One of the Savviest Guys I Ever Met—And His View on Buying Cars

When I was 20 years old, I took a summer job washing buses at a bus depot to pay for my college tuition. What I learned there from an insightful mechanic was more valuable than anything I learned at college. Russ Perry was a millionaire mechanic raising two kids as a single dad. His financial acumen was revered by the other mechanics who told me: "Hey, if Russ ever wants to talk to you about money, make sure you listen."

We worked the night shift together, which wasn't particularly busy—especially on weekends—so we had plenty of time to talk.

My job was pretty simple. I washed buses, fueled them, and recorded their mileage at the end of the day. During my free moments at work I alternated between cringing and laughing out loud when Russ sermonized about money and people. Not everything Russ had to say was politically correct, but his crassness always had an element of truth to it.

Russ claimed he could tell how smart someone was by looking at what they drove. He couldn't figure out why anyone would pay a lot of money for something—such as a luxury car—that depreciated in value over time. And if they leased it, or borrowed money to buy it, he was really left scratching his head. Russ believed in investing in assets such as houses or stocks that could appreciate over time. Anything destined to lose money, such as cars, he deemed a liability.

"Andrew," he said, "if you can go through life without losing money on cars, you're going to have a huge advantage." He pointed to the guy across the parking lot who worked in management. "You see that guy getting into that BMW?"

I admired the car when I arrived at work that night. It was a beauty. "He bought that car two years ago, brand new," Russ said. "But he has already lost $17,000 on it from depreciation and loan-interest costs. And in about three years, he's probably going to buy another one." I wondered what the car would be worth in three years, if it had already depreciated so much in just two.

"If you're truly wealthy," Russ explained, "then there's nothing wrong with blowing money you can afford to lose on the odd luxury item. But if you're trying to become wealthy," Russ said in a serious tone, "and you make those kinds of purchases, you'll never get there. Never."

Russ talked about turning conventional wisdom on its head. Most people expect to lose money on cars, but expecting it becomes a self-fulfilling prophecy. He told me that people don't have to lose money on cars if they're careful, citing himself as proof. I expected that from someone both financially and mechanically inclined. My biggest question at the time was whether it could work for me—a guy about as mechanically gifted as a blind Neanderthal with two left hands.

"When you buy a car," Russ said, "think about the resale value." The bulk of the depreciation on a new vehicle occurs in the first year. Russ recommended I never buy new cars, and only buy a car if someone else had covered the bulk of the depreciation.

The best resale value, he figured, came from Japanese cars. He recommended that I look for low-mileage models that had been fastidiously maintained with original paint, great tires, and a great interior.

If I paid the right price for a car, and the bulk of the depreciation was covered by someone else, he preached, I would be able to sell the car a year or two later for the same price I paid, if not a bit more.

A future millionaire's car-buying strategies

Putting Russ's theory to the test, I went out in search of cars that wouldn't put holes in the bottom of my financial bucket.

It didn't take me long to get a feel for the market. I read a few consumer reports on reliable automobiles. One invaluable source was Phil Edmonston's annually updated guide, *Lemon-Aid Used Cars*. Certain cars and models are bona fide lemons while others can be great little workhorses. I would spend a few minutes each morning looking through the classifieds in the local paper and when I saw something interesting at a good price, I would check it out. Over the next few years, I bought several low-mileage, reliable Japanese models, paying between $1,500 to $5,000 for a car and driving it for at least 12 months without putting any extra money into it. My cars were cheap, so my profits didn't amount to much: usually $800 to $1,000 a car.

Unfortunately there are too many people who aren't good with their money, and it's often easy to find desperate people who have overextended themselves financially. Buy from them. Generally, they want money quickly, either to upgrade their cars or to pay off oppressively looming debts. I've bought used vehicles from both types of sellers, put as many as 60,000 miles on the cars, and then sold them two or three years later for the same price I paid.

On one occasion, I bought a low-mileage, 12-year-old Toyota van for $3,000. I drove it 4,000 miles from British Columbia, Canada, down the Mexican Baja peninsula, then on to Guadalajara, before driving back to Canada. After covering more than 8,000 miles in a single trip, I sold it for $3,500. Using prudent purchasing strategies you can turn the savings into a small fortune by investing the money in ways that I'll explain later in this book.

Here's one surprisingly simple strategy for buying used vehicles that can save you loads of time and money.

Imagine wandering onto a car lot. You're not generally given free rein to browse on your own or with a friend. A sharply dressed salesperson will soon be courting you through a variety of makes and models. They could have the very best of intentions, but if you're anything like me, your pulse will race a bit faster as you're shadowed, and the pressure of being shadowed by a slick talker might throw you off. After all, you're on their turf.

A minnow like me needs an effective strategy against big, hungry, experienced fish—and this is mine: First, I identify exactly what I'm looking for. In 2002, I wanted a Japanese car with a stick shift and original paint. I didn't want a new paint job because I'm not skilled enough to determine whether something had been covered up, such as rust or damage from an accident. I also wanted to ensure that the car had fewer than 80,000 miles on it, and I wanted to pay less than $3,000. It really didn't matter how old the car was as long as it had been properly maintained and hadn't been around the block too many times.

Like a secret agent wrapped up in the bravery of anonymity, I pulled out my hit list from the yellow pages to call every car lot within a 20-mile radius. Sticking to my guns, I told them exactly what I was looking for and wouldn't entertain anything that didn't fit all of my criteria.

I did have to hold my ground with aggressive sales staff. But it was a lot easier to do over the telephone than it would have been in person. Most of the dealers told me that they had something I would be interested in, but they couldn't go as low as $3,000. Some tried tempting me into their lairs with alternatives; others referred to my price ceiling as delusional. But I wasn't bothered. My strategy was a knight's sword and the phone, my trusty shield. I also practiced chivalry—knowing that I might end up calling on them again.

Because my first round of phone calls didn't pan out, I called the dealers back when it got closer to the end of the month. I hoped the salespeople would be hungrier by then to meet their monthly quotas. As fortune would have it, at one dealership an elderly couple had traded in an older Toyota Tercel with 30,000 miles on it. The car hadn't been cleaned or inspected, but the dealership was willing to do a quick turnaround sale for $3,000.

This strategy doesn't have to be limited to a $3,000 purchase. The process makes sense for any make or model and it saves time. What's more, the money you save can be effectively invested to build wealth.

Careful Home Purchases

Most people realize that expensive automobile purchases can hinder wealth. But the global financial crisis of 2008–2009 taught us important lessons about homes as well.

One of the lessons aspiring rich people have to learn is that the banks aren't really their friends. They're out to make money for their shareholders. To do so, they often hire the kindest or most convincing salespeople they can to persuade you to buy lousy investment products (which I'll discuss in Chapter 3) while sugar-coating bloated house loans to keep you paying too many years of interest.

What caused the financial crisis of 2008–2009? The greed of the banks not looking after the best interests of their customers, coupled with the ignorance of those who bought homes they couldn't afford.

Caught up in the housing boom, buyers purchased homes they couldn't really pay for, and when the dangerously enticing, low interest rates finally rose, they couldn't make their mortgage payments. Unsurprisingly, many were forced to sell their homes, creating a surplus in the housing market. When there's a surplus of anything, people aren't willing to pay as much for those items—so they fall in price. Houses were no exception.

The banks had sold these mortgage loans to other institutions around the world. But when the original holders of the mortgages (the home purchasers) couldn't afford their mortgage payments, the financial institutions repossessed their houses—but at a significant loss, because housing prices were falling like a skydiver without a chute.

The banks had also bundled the loans up and sold them to other global institutions, which were then on the hook when the homeowners couldn't pay their mortgages, putting many of the world's most respected financial institutions in peril. With dwindling financial resources, the banks didn't loan as readily to other businesses, which in turn didn't have the funds to cover their day-to-day operations. The snowball effect resulted in a global slowdown and mass layoffs. Don't believe those who sugarcoat housing loans. The effects can be devastating.

It reminds me of a lesson my mom taught me when I took out my first mortgage on a piece of oceanfront land. She asked me: "If the interest rate doubled, could you still afford to make the payment?" According to the terms of the mortgage, I was being charged seven percent in interest a year. She knew at the time, that a seven percent mortgage was historically cheap, especially compared with mortgage rates in the late 1970s and 1980s. As far as she was concerned, if I couldn't afford to pay double, or 14 percent interest, then rising interest rates could expose me. I would be one of those unfortunate guys caught swimming naked when the tide goes out.

Her advice is a good rule of thumb if you don't want to be stripped of your real estate. If you're considering purchasing a home, double the interest rate and figure out if you could still afford the payments. If you can, then you can afford the home.

Millionaire Handouts

There's a Chinese proverb suggesting that wealth doesn't last more than three generations. There's a generation that builds wealth, a generation that maintains it, and a generation that squanders it.

U.S. studies suggest that—contrary to what we might think—most millionaires didn't inherit their wealth. More than 80 percent of those surveyed are first-generation rich.[10]

I teach at a private school in Singapore where most of the expat students come from affluent families. I tell my students (only half-jokingly) that they're on the financial endangered species list. It's natural for parents to want to help their children. But the Chinese have known for thousands of years what happens to money that's given to youngsters who had no hand in building that wealth. It gets squandered.

In Thomas Stanley's classic book, *The Millionaire Next Door,* he explains that adults who receive "helpful" financial gifts from their parents (stocks, cash, real estate) typically end up with lower levels of wealth than people in the same income bracket who don't receive financial assistance.[11]

It's a tough concept for many parents to grasp. They feel they can give their kids a strong financial head start by giving them money. Statistically speaking, easy money is wasted money. Stanley studied a broad cross section of educated professionals in their 40s and 50s, and he categorized them by vocation. Then he split them up into two groups: those who had received financial assistance from their parents, and those who hadn't. That assistance included cash gifts, help in paying off loans, help in buying a car, or help with a down payment on a home. He found that those who received help were more likely to have less wealth during their peak earning years than those who had not received financial help from their parents. Receiving financial handouts hinders a person's ability to create wealth.

For example, the average accountant who received financial help from his or her parents was 43 percent less wealthy than an average accountant who didn't receive handouts. In sharp contrast, the only two professional groups studied that became wealthier after receiving financial assistance were school teachers and college professors.[12]

How Did I Become a Millionaire?

My dad was a mechanic, and I was one of four kids being raised on his salary, so we didn't have a lot of money to throw around when I was growing up. From the age of 15, I bought my own clothes. At 16, I bought my own car with earnings from a part-time job at a supermarket. I had to work for what I wanted, but I didn't enjoy working. Like most kids, I would have preferred hanging out on a beach.

So for me, money was equated with work. I would see a desired object costing "just" $10, but then I would ask myself if I wanted to mop the supermarket floor and stack 50-pound sacks of potatoes to pay for it. If the answer was no, then I wouldn't buy it. Never receiving "free" money allowed me to adopt responsible spending habits.

Confessions of a former cheapskate

Today, my wife and I can afford to live well. We own a classic Mercedes-Benz and a utilitarian Mazda. We travel prolifically, having visited more than 25 different countries. We live in a luxurious condominium with a swimming pool, squash courts, tennis courts, and a weight room. We enjoy massages every week, 52 weeks a year. If our health holds out, we'll enjoy these fruits for the next 40 years.

But an early aversion to debt put us in this position. I hate debt. It's going to sound extreme to most people, but for me, owing money is like making a deal with the devil. Always thinking of the

worry what would happen if I lost my
:bt-obligation payments.
; that a young person seeking early
vay I did in my early 20s. But thinking
;, contagious disease served me pretty
spirational or delusional, I think you'll

h grade a few months after graduating
rent and low food costs, I figured, were
n obliteration. Sure, it sounds like a rea-
big-city panhandlers who might cringe

Potatoes, pasta, and clams were the cheapest forms of suste-
nance I could find. Clams simply represented free protein. With a
bucket in hand, I would wander to the beach with a retired fellow named Oscar, and we would load up on clams. While Oscar
turned his catch into delicacies, my efforts were spartan: micro-
wave some spuds or boil pasta, and toss in the clams with a bit
of olive oil. *Voila!* Dinner for less than a dollar. It doesn't matter
how well you can initially tolerate a bland meal. Keeping that diet
up day after day is about as enticing as eating dog food. But my
debt burden lessened as I lived on just 30 percent of my teacher's
salary—allowing me to allocate 70 percent of my salary toward
debt reduction.

Sharing accommodation with roommates also cut costs. I preferred, however, not paying rent at all, so I looked for people escap-
ing to the Sunbelt for winter and needed someone to look after
their homes for the season.

No matter how cold the rent-free homes got during the winter,
I never turned on the heat. Wanting to keep costs down, I would
walk around the house wearing layers of shirts and sweaters while
the winter's snow piled up outside. If there was a fireplace, I used
it. At night, I would make a roaring fire and then drag blankets in
front of it to sleep. Waking up during winter mornings, I often saw
my breath.

One December week, my father was in town on business, so
I invited him to stay with me. Typically boisterous, he was unchar-
acteristically quiet when I told him: "No Dad, I'm not going to turn
on the heat." I figured that snuggling up together at night next to a

fireplace in a frosty living room would be a great father-son bonding moment. I guess he didn't think so. The next time he was in town, he stayed at a hotel.

Eventually, I craved the freedom of my own place, so I moved into a basement suite where the landlord charged $350 a month. But low rents can come with inconveniences. In this case, I was a long way from the school where I taught—35 miles door to door.

If I had been smart enough to drive a car to work, it wouldn't have been so bad. I owned a rusting, 20-year-old Volkswagen that I bought for $1,200 (which I sold two years later for $1,800), but I wasn't prepared to pay fuel prices for the 70-mile round-trip commute. So . . . I rode my bike.

Riding an old mountain bike 70 miles a day through rain and sleet on my way to work and back gave me a frontrunner's edge for the bonehead award. At the time, I had an investment portfolio that would have allowed me to buy a brand-new sports car in cash, if I had wanted to, and I could have rented an oceanside apartment. But the people I worked with probably thought I was broke.

One of my fellow teachers saw me at a gas station on my way home from work. We were both picking up fuel—but mine was of the edible kind. Rushing up to me as I straddled my bike and stuffed a PowerBar into my mouth she said: "We should really start a collection for you at the school, Andrew." If I thought she was kidding, I would have laughed.

After a while, even I decided my lifestyle was a little extreme. To make things easier, I moved closer to work after placing an advertisement in the local paper: *Teacher looking for accommodation for no more than $450 a month*. It was far below the going rate, but I reasoned an advertisement selling myself as employed and responsible—while leaving out a few other adjectives—might attract someone looking for a dependable tenant.

I only got a couple of calls but one of the places was perfect, so I took it.

Because I had been investing money since I was 19, I already had a growing nest egg. But I wasn't willing to sell any of my investments to pay down my loans. I threw every extra income dollar I could toward reducing my student loans. One year after working full-time and living like a monk, I paid off my debts. Then I redirected the money enthusiastically into my investments.

Six years after paying off my student loans, I bought a piece of oceanfront property and calculated how to aggressively pay down the mortgage. I even took a higher interest rate to increase my flexibility of mortgage payments.

Once I paid it off, I shoveled money, once again, into my investments.

Admittedly, few people despise debt as much as I do. But once you're debt-free, there's no feeling like it.

Don't get me wrong. This part of my financial history isn't a "how to" manual for a young person to follow. It was a fun challenge at the time, but it wouldn't appeal to me today. And my wife, who I married much later, admits it wouldn't have appealed to her—ever. That said, if you want to be wealthy, you dramatically increase your odds if you're frugal, especially when you're young.

Looking to the Future

Responsible spending habits are often overlooked by people who want to be rich. It's one of the reasons many people nearing retirement age have to work when they would rather be traveling the world or spending time with their grandchildren. Naturally, not everyone has the same philosophy about work. But how many people on their deathbeds ever lament: "Gosh, I wish I had spent more time at the office," or "Geez, I really wish they had given me that promotion back in 2015."

Most people prefer their hobbies to their workplace, their children to their BlackBerries, and their quiet reflective moments to their office meetings. I'm certainly among them—which is the reason I learned to control my spending and invest my money effectively.

If you're a young person starting out and you see someone with the latest expensive toys, think about how they might have acquired them. Too many of those items were probably bought on credit—with sleepless nights as a complementary accessory. Many of those people will never truly be rich. Instead, they will be stressed.

By learning how to spend like a rich person, you can eventually build wealth (and material possessions) without the added anxiety. You don't have to live like a pauper to do it either. Apply the investment rules that I'm willing to share, and you could feasibly invest half of what your neighbor does, take lower risks, and still end up with twice as much money as they do. Read on to find out how.

Notes

1. Kelli B. Grant, "The New Best Credit Cards," *The Wall Street Journal*, April 1, 2011, accessed April 2, 2011, http://www.marketwatch .com/story/the-new-best-credit-cards-1301520786753.
2. Derek Kravitz, "Number of Underwater Mortgages Rise as More Homeowners Fall Behind," *The Huffington Post*, March 8, 2011, accessed April 2, 2011, http://www.huffingtonpost.com/2011 /03/08/number-of-underwater-mort_n_833000.html.
3. Thomas Stanley, *Stop Acting Rich* (Hoboken, New Jersey: John Wiley & Sons, 2009), 9.
4. Ibid., 45.
5. "Household Income for States: 2008 and 2009," U.S. Census Bureau, accessed April 2, 2011, http://www.census.gov/prod/ 2010pubs/acsbr09-2.pdf.
6. Dave Feschuk, "NBA Players' Financial Security No Slam Dunk," *Toronto Star,* January 31, 2008, accessed April 2, 2011, http:// www.thestar.com/sports/article/299119.
7. Stanley, *Stop Acting Rich*, 204.
8. Ibid.
9. "Warren Buffett Vouches for GM with Caddy Purchase," LeftLane, June 6, 2006, accessed October 2010, http://www.leftlanenews .com/warren-buffett-vouches-for-gm-with-caddy-purchase.html.
10. Stanley, *Stop Acting Rich*, 204.
11. Thomas Stanley and William Danko, *The Millionaire Next Door* (New York, New York: Simon & Schuster, 1996), 9.
12. Ibid., 151.

RULE 2
Use the Greatest Investment Ally You Have

So much of what schools teach in a traditional mathematics class is . . . hmm, let me word this diplomatically, not likely to affect our day-to-day lives. Sure, learning the formulas for quadratic equations (and their abstract family members) might jazz the odd engineering student. But let's be honest. Few people get aroused by quadratic equations.

Perhaps I'm committing heresy in the eyes of the world's math teachers, but I think quadratic equations (a polynomial equation of the second degree, if that clears things up) are about as useful to most people as ingrown toenails and just as painful for some. Having said that, buried in the dull pages of most school math books is something that's actually useful: the magical premise of compound interest.

Warren Buffett applied it to become a billionaire. More importantly, so can you and I'll show you how.

Buffett has long jockeyed with Microsoft Chairman Bill Gates for the title of "World's Richest Man." He lives like a typical millionaire (he doesn't spend much on material things) and he mastered the secret of investing his money early. He bought his first stock when he was 11 years old, and the multibillionaire jokes that he started too late.[1]

Starting early is the greatest gift you can give yourself. If you start early and if you invest efficiently (in a manner that I'll explain in this book) you can build a fortune over time, while spending just 60 minutes a year monitoring your investments.

Warren Buffett famously quips:"Preparation is everything. Noah did not start building the Ark when it was raining."[2]

Most of us are aware of the Biblical story about Noah's Ark. God told him to build an Ark and to collect a variety of animals, and eventually, when the rains came, they would sail off to a new beginning. Luckily for the animals, Noah started building that Ark right away. He didn't procrastinate.

But let's imagine Noah for a second. The guy probably had a similar nature to you and me, so even if God told him to keep the upcoming flood a secret, he might not have. After all, he was human too. So I can imagine him wandering down to the local watering hole and after having a couple of forerunners to Budweiser beer, whispering to a friend: "Hey listen, God is saying that the rains are going to come and that I have to build an Ark and sail away once the land is flooded." Some of his buddies (maybe even all of them) might have figured Noah had accidently eaten some kind of naturally grown narcotic. A crazy story they would think.

Yet, someone must have believed him. As far-fetched as Noah's flood story might have sounded to his buddies, it would have inspired at least one of his friends to build his own Ark—or at least a decent-sized boat.

Despite the best of intentions, though, that person obviously never got around to it. Maybe he planned to build it when he acquired more money to pay for the materials. Maybe he wanted to be sure, waiting to see if the clouds grew dark and it started sprinkling. English naturalist Charles Darwin might call this guy's procrastination "natural selection." Needless to say, he wasn't selected.

For the best odds of amassing wealth in the stock and bond markets, it's best to start early.

Thankfully your friends—if they procrastinate—won't meet the same fate as Noah's friends, but your metaphorical ship will sail off into the distance while others scramble in the rain to assemble their own boats.

Starting early is more than just getting a head start. It's about using magic. You can sail away slowly, and your friends can come after you with racing boats. But thanks to the force described by Albert Einstein (some say) as more powerful than splitting the atom, they aren't likely to catch you.

In William Shakespeare's *Hamlet*, the protagonist says to his friend: "There are more things in heaven and earth, Horatio, than are dreamt of in your philosophy."

Hamlet was referring to ghosts. Einstein was referring to the magic of compound interest.

Compound Interest—The World's Most Powerful Financial Concept

Compound interest might sound like a complicated process, but it's simple.

If $100 attracts 10 percent interest in one year, then we know that it gained $10, turning $100 into $110.

You would start the second year with $110, and if it increases 10 percent, it would gain $11, turning $110 into $121.

You will go into the third year with $121 in your pocket, and if it increases 10 percent, it would gain $12.10, turning $121 into $133.10.

It isn't long before a snowball effect takes place. Have a look at what $100 invested at 10 percent annually can do.

$100 at 10 percent compounding interest a year turns into—

- $161.05 after 5 years

- $259.37 after 10 years

- $417.72 after 15 years

- $672.74 after 20 years

- $1,744.94 after 30 years

- $4,525.92 after 40 years

- $11,739.08 after 50 years

- $78,974.69 after 70 years

- $204,840.02 after 80 years

- $1,378,061.23 after 100 years

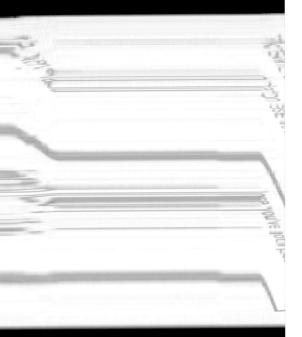

Some of the lengthier periods above might look dramatically unrealistic. But you don't have to be a creepy, ageless character in the *Twilight* series to benefit. Someone who starts investing at 19 (like I did) and who lives until they're 90 (which I hope to!) will have money compounding in the markets for 71 years. They will spend some of it along the way, but they'll always want to keep a portion of their money compounding in case they live to 100.

The inspirational realities of starting early

After paying off your high interest loans (whether they are car loans or credit-card loans) you will be ready to put Buffett's Noah Principle to work. The earlier you start, the better—so if you're 18 years old, start now. If you're 50 years old, and you haven't begun, there's no better time than the present. You'll never be younger than you are right now.

The money that doesn't go toward expensive cars, the latest tech gadgets, and credit-card payments (assuming you have paid off your credit debts) can compound dramatically in the stock market if you're patient. And the longer your money is invested in the stock market, the lower the risk.

We know that stock markets can fluctuate dramatically. They can even move sideways for many years. But over the past 90 years, the U.S. stock market has generated returns exceeding nine percent annually.[3] This includes the crashes of 1929, 1973–1974, 1987, and 2008–2009. In *Stocks for the Long Run*, University of Pennsylvania's Wharton School finance professor Jeremy Siegel suggests a dominant historical market, such as the U.S., isn't the only source of impressive long-term returns. Despite the shrinking global importance of England, its stock market returns since 1926 have been very similar to that of the U.S. Meanwhile, not even two devastating world wars for Germany have hurt its long-term stock market performance, which also rivals that of the United States.[4]

My suggestion isn't going to be to choose one country's stock market over another. Some stock markets will do better than others, but without mythical crystal balls we're not going to know ahead of time. Instead, to ensure the best chances of success, owning an interest in all of the world's stock markets is a good idea. And you can benefit exponentially by investing as early as you can. The younger you are when you start investing, the better.

Grow wealthier than your neighbor while investing less

The question below showcases how powerful the "Noah Principle" of starting early really is.

A. Would you rather invest $32,400 and turn it into $1,050,180? Or,

B. Would you rather invest $240,000 and turn it into $813,128?

Sure it's a dumb question. Anyone who can fog a mirror would choose A. But because most people haven't had a strong financial education, the vast majority would be lucky to face scenario B— never mind scenario A.

If you know anyone who's really young, they can benefit from your knowledge. They can feasibly turn $32,400 into more than a million dollars. But don't weaken them by giving them money. *Make them earn it.* Here's how it can be done.

The Bohemian Millionaire—The Best of Historical-Based Fiction

A five-year-old girl named Star is raised by her mother, Autumn, and brought up on a Bohemian island where the locals make their own clothes, where neither men nor women use razors to shave, and where no one tries to mask the aphrodisiac quality of good old-fashioned sweat.

Unfortunately, despite how appealing this might sound (especially at tightly congested town hall meetings) it isn't paradise. Islanders and locals alike often throw empty aluminum beverage cans into ditches. Autumn convinces Star that collecting those cans and recycling them can help the environment and eventually make her a millionaire. Autumn takes Star to the local recycling depot where Star collects an average of $1.45 a day from refunded cans and bottles. Although a Bohemian at heart, Autumn's no provincial bumpkin. She recognizes that if she persuades Star to earn $1.45 a day from can returns, she can invest the daily $1.45 to make Star a millionaire.

Putting it into the U.S. stock market, Star earns an average of nine percent a year (which is slightly less than what the stock market has averaged over the past 90 years). Autumn also understands what most parents do not: If she teaches Star to save, her daughter will become a financial powerhouse. But if she "gifts" Star money, rather than coaching her to earn it, then her daughter may become financially inept.

Fast forward 20 years. Star is now 25 years old, and although she no longer collects cans from ditches, her mother insists Star sends her a $45 monthly check (roughly $1.45 per day). Autumn continues to invest Star's money while Star hawks her handmade Dream Catchers at the local farmer's market.

Living in New York City, Star's best friend Lucy works as an investment banker. (I know you're wondering how these two hooked up, but roll with it. It's my story.) Living the "good life," Lucy drives a BMW, dines at gourmet restaurants and blows the rest of her significant income on clothing, theater shows, expensive shoes, and flashy jewelry.

At age 40, Lucy begins to save $800 a month, and she gets on Star's case, via e-mail, about Star's limited $45-a-month contribution to her financial future.

Star doesn't want to brag but she needs to set Lucy straight.

"Lucy," she writes, "you're the one in financial trouble, not me. It's true that you're investing far more money than I am, but you'll need to invest more than $800 a month if you want as much as I'll have when I retire."

The e-mail puzzles Lucy, who assumes that Star must have ingested some very Bohemian mushrooms to write such cryptic nonsense.

Twenty-five years later, both women are 65 years old, and they decide to rent a retirement home together in Lake Chapala, Mexico, where their money would go a lot further.

"Well, inquires Star, "Did you invest more than $800 a month like I suggested?"

"This is coming from someone investing $45 a month?" asks Lucy with surprise.

"But Lucy, you ignored the Noah principle, so despite investing far more money, you ended up with a lot less than I did because you started investing so much later."

Both women achieved the same return in the stock market. Some years they gained money, other years they lost money, but overall, they each averaged nine percent.

Figure 2.1 shows that because Star started early, she was able to invest a total of $32,400 and turn it into more than $1 million. Lucy started later, invested nearly eight times more, but ended up with $237,052 less than Star.

I didn't start investing until I was 19, so Star would have had the jump on me. But I started far earlier than most, so I have had more time to let the Noah Principle work its magic. I put money in U.S. and international stock markets that, from 1990 to 2011, have averaged more than 10 percent annually. The money I put in the market in 1990 is now seven times its original value.

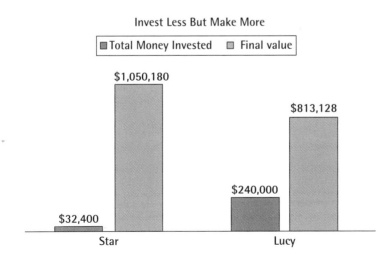

Figure 2.1   Turning Less into More

When I tell young parents about the power of compounding money, they're often inspired to set aside money for their children's future. "Setting aside" money for a child, however, is very different from encouraging a child to earn, save, and invest.

Giving money promotes weakness and dependence.

Teaching money lessons and cheerleading the struggle promotes strength, independence, and pride.

Gifting Money to Yourself

In 2005, I was having dinner with a couple of school teachers, and the topic of savings came up. They wanted to know how much they should save for their retirement. Unlike most public school teachers, who can look forward to pensions when they retire, these friends are in the same boat that I'm in: as private school teachers, they're responsible for their own retirement money.

I threw out a minimum dollar figure that I thought they should save each month. It was double what they were currently saving.

The woman (who I'll call Julie) thought it was an attainable amount. Her husband (who I'll call Tom) thought it was crazy. So I asked them to do a couple of things:

1. Write down everything they spent money on for three months, including food costs, mortgage costs, gas for the car, and health insurance.

2. At the end of those three months, figure out what it cost them to live each month.

The next time we had dinner together, they told me their results, which had given them both a jolt. Julie was surprised at how much she was spending on eating out, buying clothes, and purchasing small items such as Starbucks coffee.

Tom was surprised at how much he was spending on beers at the clubhouse when he went golfing with his buddies.

As the three-month period progressed, an awakening took place. Pulling receipts from their wallets and writing down their expenses each evening made them realize how much they were squandering.

As Tom explained: "I knew that I had to write those purchases down at the end of the day, which acted as an accountability measurement. So I started spending less."

Financially efficient households know what their costs are. By writing down expenses, two things generally occur. You get an idea of how much you spend in a month, providing an idea of how much you can invest. It also makes you accountable for your spending, which encourages most people to cut back.

The next step is to figure out exactly what you get paid in the average month.

When you subtract your average monthly expense costs from your income, you can get an idea of how much you can afford to invest. Don't wait until the end of the month to invest that money; instead, make the transfer payment to your investment of choice on the day you get paid. Otherwise, you might not have enough left at the end of the month (after a few too many nights out) to follow through with your new financial plan. My wife made that mistake before we were married, investing whatever amount she had left in her account at the end of the month or the end of the year. When she switched things around and automatically had money transferred from her savings account on the date she was paid, she ended up investing twice as much.

My friends Julie and Tom had the same realization. After a year, they had doubled the amount that they were investing. Two years later when the same conversation came up, I found they had tripled the amount they were originally putting away. Both said the same thing: "We didn't know where that money was going each month. It doesn't feel like we live any differently than we did three years ago, but the deposits in our investment account don't lie. We've tripled our savings."

After a while, you probably won't have to write down every penny you spend. You'll fall into a healthy spending pattern, and the money that gets transferred automatically to your investment account can grow over time.

Here's another useful tip. Over the years, your salary will most likely rise. If it increases by $1,000 in a given year, add at least half of it to your investment account, while putting the rest in a separate account for something special. That way, you'll get rewarded twice for the salary increase.

When You Definitely Shouldn't Invest

Before getting wrapped up in how much money you can save and invest, there's one very important thing you need to clear up. Are you paying interest on credit cards? If you are, then it makes no financial sense to invest money. Most credit cards charge 18 to 24 percent in interest annually. Not paying them off in full at the end of the month means that your friendly card company (the one you'll never leave home without) is sucking your money from an intravenous drip attached to your femoral artery. You don't have to be smarter than a fifth grader to realize that paying 18 percent interest on credit-card debt and investing money that you hope will provide returns of 10 percent makes as much sense as bathing fully clothed in a giant tub of Vaseline and then travelling home on the roof of a bus.

Paying off credit-card debt that's charging 18 percent in interest is like making a tax-free 18 percent gain on your money. And there's no way that your investments can guarantee a gain like that after tax. If any financial adviser, advertisement, or investment group of any kind promises a return of 18 percent annually, think of disgraced U.S. financier Bernie Madoff and run. Nobody can guarantee those kinds of returns.

Well, nobody except the credit-card companies. They're making 18 to 24 percent annually *from* you (if you carry a balance), not *for* you.

How and Why Stocks Rise in Value

You might be wondering how I averaged 10 percent a year on the stock market for 20 years. There were certainly years when my money dropped in value, but there were years when I earned a lot more than 10 percent as well.

Where does the money come from? How is it created?

Imagine Willy Wonka (from Roald Dahl's classic novel, *Charlie and the Chocolate Factory*) starting off with a little chocolate shop. Having big dreams, he wanted to make ice cream that didn't melt, chewing gum that never lost its flavor, and chocolate that would make even the devil sell his soul.

But Willy didn't have enough money to grow his factory. He needed to buy a larger building, hire more of those creepy little workers, and purchase machinery that would make chocolate faster than he ever could before.

So Willy hired someone to approach the New York Stock Exchange and before Willy knew it, he had investors in his business. They bought parts of his business, also known as "shares" or "stock." Willy was no longer the sole owner, but by selling part of his business to new shareholders, he was able to build a larger, more efficient factory with the shareholder proceeds, which increased the chocolate factory's profits because he was able to make more treats at a faster rate.

Willy's company was now "public," meaning that the shareowners (should they choose to) could sell their stakes in Willy's company to other willing buyers. When a publicly traded company has shares that trade on a stock market, the trading activity has a negligible effect on the business. So Willy, of course, was able to concentrate on what he did best: making chocolate. The shareholders didn't bother him because generally, minority shareholders don't have any influence in a company's day-to-day operations.

Willy's chocolate was amazing. Pleasing the shareholders, he began selling more and more chocolate. But they wanted more than a certificate from the New York Stock Exchange or their local brokerage firm proving they were partial owners of the chocolate factory. They wanted to share in the business profits that the factory generated. This made sense because shareholders in a company are technically owners.

So the board of directors (which was voted into their positions by the shareholders) decided to give the owners an annual percentage of the profits, known as a dividend, and everyone was happy. This is how it worked: Willy's factory sold about $100,000 worth of chocolate and goodies each year. After paying taxes on the earnings, employee wages, and maintenance costs, Willy Wonka's Chocolate Factory made year-to-year profit of $10,000, so the company's board of directors decided to pay its shareholders $5,000 of that annual $10,000 profit and split it among the shareholders. This is known as a dividend.

The remaining $5,000 profit would be reinvested back into the business—so Willy could pay for bigger and better machinery, advertise his chocolate far and wide, and make chocolate even faster, generating higher profits.

Those reinvested profits made Willy's business even more lucrative. As a result, the Chocolate Factory doubled its profits to $20,000 the following year, and it increased its dividend payout to shareholders.

This of course caused other potential investors to drool. They wanted to buy shares in the factory too. Now there were more people wanting to buy shares than there were people who wanted to sell them. This created a demand for the shares, causing the share price on the New York Stock Exchange to rise. (If there are more buyers than sellers, the share price rises. If there are more sellers than buyers, the share price falls.)

Over time, the share price of Willy's business fluctuated: sometimes climbing, sometimes falling, depending on investor sentiment. If news about the company was good, it increased public demand for the shares, pushing up the price. On other days, investors grew pessimistic, causing the share price to fall.

Willy's factory continued to make more money over the years. And over the long term, when a company increases its profits, the stock price generally rises along with it.

Willy's shareholders were able to make money in two different ways. They could realize a profit from dividends (cash payments given to shareholders usually four times each year) or they could wait until their stock had increased substantially in value on the stock market and choose to sell some or all of their shares.

Here's how an investor could hypothetically make 10 percent a year from owning shares in Willy Wonka's business:

Montgomery Burns had his eye on Willy Wonka's Chocolate Factory shares, and he decided to buy $1,000 of the chocolate company's stock at $10 a share. After one year, if the share price rose to $10.50, this would amount to a five percent increase in the share price ($10.50 is five percent higher than the $10 that Burns paid).

And if Burns was given a $50 dividend, we could say that he had earned an additional five percent because a $50 dividend is five percent of his initial $1,000 investment.

So if his shares gain five percent in value from the share-price increase and he makes an extra five percent from the dividend payment, then after one year Burns potentially would have made a

10 percent profit on his shares. Of course, only the five percent dividend payout would go into his pocket as a "realized" profit. The five percent "profit" from the price appreciation (as the stock rose in value) would only be realized if Burns sold his Willy Wonka shares.

Montgomery Burns, however, didn't become the richest man in Springfield by buying and selling Willy Wonka shares when they fluctuated in price. Studies have shown that, on average, investors who buy shares and sell them again quickly don't tend to make profits as high as investors who hold onto their shares over the long term.

Burns held onto those shares for many years. Sometimes the share price rose and sometimes it fell. But the company kept increasing its profits, so the share price increased over time. The annual dividends kept a smile on Montgomery Burns' greedy little lips, as his profits from the rising stock price coupled with dividends earned him an average potential return of 10 percent a year.

However, Burns wasn't rubbing his bony hands together as gleefully as you might expect because at the same time he bought Willy Wonka shares, he also bought shares in Homer's donuts and Lou's bar. Neither business worked out, and Burns lost money.

Driving him really crazy, however, was missing out on shares in the joke-store company, Bart's Barf Gags. If Burns had bought shares in this business, he would be laughing—all the way to the bank. Share prices quadrupled in just four years.

In the following chapter, I will show you that one of the best ways to invest in the stock market is to own every stock in the market, rather than trying to follow the strategy of Burns and guess which stocks will rise. Though it sounds impossible to buy virtually every stock in a given market, it's made easy by purchasing a single product that owns every stock within it.

Before getting to that, remember that you can invest half of what your neighbors invest over your lifetime and still end up with twice as much money—if you start early enough. For patient investors, the aggregate returns of the world's stock markets have dished out phenomenal profits.

For example, the U.S. stock market has averaged 9.96 percent annually from 1920 to 2010. There were periods where it grew faster than that, while it dropped back at other times. But that 9.96 percent average return, as shown in Table 2.1, has provided some impressive

Table 2.1   How $1,000 Would Grow Over Time If It Made 9.96% Annually

Years of Growth	Value
0	$1,000
10	$2,584.32
20	$6,678.74
30	$17,260.04
40	$44,604.58
50	$115,275.37
60	$297,909.16
70	$769,894.43
80	$1,989,658.28
90	$5,141,925.80

Source: The Value Line Investment Survey; Morningstar

long-term profits. Invest early, and invest frequently. The odds are high that you'll slowly grow very wealthy. Let me show you how.

Notes

1. Jay Steele, *Warren Buffett, Master of the Market* (New York: Avon Books, 1999), 17.
2. Andrew Kilpatrick, *Of Permanent Value, The Story of Warren Buffett* (Birmingham, Alabama: Andy Kilpatrick Publishing Empire, 2006), 226.
3. The Value Line Investment Survey—A Long-Term Perspective Chart 1920–2005 and Morningstar Performance Tracking of DOW Jones ETF from 2005 to 2011.
4. Jeremy Siegel, *Stocks for The Long Run*, 3rd ed. (New York: McGraw-Hill, 2002), 18.

RULE 3
Small Percentages Pack Big Punches

In 1971, when the great boxer Muhammad Ali was still undefeated, U.S. basketball star Wilt Chamberlain suggested publicly that he stood a chance beating Ali in the boxing ring. Promoters scrambled to organize a fight that Ali considered a joke. Whenever the ultraconfident Ali walked into a room with the towering Chamberlain within earshot, he would cup his hands and holler through them: "Timber-r-r-r-r!"

While Chamberlain felt that one lucky punch could knock Ali out and that he stood a decent chance in a fight, the rest of the sporting world knew better. Chamberlain's odds of winning were ridiculously low, and his bravado could only lead to significant pain for the great basketball player.

As legend has it, Ali's "Timber-r-r-r-r!" taunts eventually rattled Chamberlain's nerves to put a stop to the pending fight.[1]

Most people don't like losing, and for that reason there are certain things most of us won't do. If we're smart (sorry Wilt) we won't bet a professional boxer that we can beat him or her in the ring. We won't bet a prosecuting lawyer that we can defend ourselves in a court of law and win. We won't put our money down on the odds of beating a chess master at chess.

But would we dare challenge a professional financial adviser in a long-term investing contest? Common sense initially suggests that we shouldn't. However, this may be the only exception to the rule of challenging someone in their given profession—and beating them easily.

With Training, the Average Fifth Grader Can Take on Wall Street

The kid doesn't have to be smart. He just needs to learn that when following financial advice from most professional advisers, he won't be steered toward the best investments. The game is rigged against the average investor because most advisers make money for themselves—at their clients' expense.

The selfish reality of the financial service industry

The vast majority of financial advisers are salespeople who will put their own financial interests ahead of yours. They sell you investment products that pay them (or their employers) well, while you're a distant second on their priority list. Many of us know people who work as financial planners, and they're fun to talk to at parties or on the golf course. But if they're buying actively managed mutual funds for their clients, they're doing their clients a disservice.

Instead of recommending actively managed mutual funds (which the vast number of advisers do), they should direct their clients toward index funds.

Index funds—What experts love but advisers hate

Every nonfiction book has an index. Go ahead, flip to the back of this one and scan all those referenced words representing this book's content. A book's index is a representation of everything that's inside it.

Now think of the stock market as a book. If you went to the back pages (the index) you could see a representation of everything that was inside that "book." For example, if you went to the back pages of the U.S. stock market, you would see the names of such listed companies as Wal-Mart, The Gap, Exxon Mobil, Procter & Gamble, Colgate-Palmolive, and the directory would go on and on until several thousand businesses were named.

In the world of investing, if you buy a U.S. total stock market index fund, you're buying a single product that has thousands of stocks within it. It represents the entire U.S. stock market.

With just *three index funds*, your money can be spread over nearly every available global money basket:

1. A home country stock market index (for Americans, this would be a U.S. index; for Canadians, a Canadian stock index)

2. An international stock market index (holding the widest array of international stocks from around the world)

3. A government bond market index (money you would lend to a government for a guaranteed stable rate of interest)

I'll explain the bond index in Chapter 5, and in Chapter 6, I'll introduce you to four real people from across the globe who created indexed investment portfolios. It was easy for them (as you'll see) and it will be easy for you.

That's it. With just three index funds, you'll beat the pants (and the shirts, socks, underwear, and shoes) off most financial professionals.

Financial Experts Backing the Irrefutable

Full-time professionals in other fields, let's say dentists, bring a lot to the layman. But in aggregate, people get nothing for their money from professional money managers . . . The best way to own common stocks is through an index fund.[2]

Warren Buffett, Berkshire Hathaway Chairman

If you were to ask Warren Buffett what you should invest in, he would suggest that you buy index funds. As the world's greatest investor, and as a man slowly giving away his fortune to charity, Warren Buffett's testimony is part of his pledge to give back to society. In this case, he's giving back knowledge: be wary of the financial service industry, and invest with index funds instead.

I don't believe I would have amassed a million dollars on a teacher's salary while still in my 30s if I were unknowingly paying hidden fees to a financial adviser. Don't think I'm not a generous guy. I just don't want to be giving away hundreds of thousands of dollars during my investment lifetime to a slick talker in a salesperson's cloak. And I don't think you should either.

What would a nobel prize-winning economist suggest?

The most efficient way to diversify a stock portfolio is with a low fee index fund.[3]

Paul Samuelson, 1970 Nobel Prize in Economics

Arguably the most famous economist of our time, the late Paul Samuelson was the first American to win a Nobel Prize in Economics. It's fair to say that he knew a heck of a lot more about money than the brokers suffering from conflicts of interest at your neighborhood Merrill Lynch, Edward Jones, or Raymond James offices.

The typical financial planner won't want you knowing this, but a dream team of Economic Nobel Laureates clarifies that advisers and individuals who think they can beat the stock market indexes are likely to be wrong time after time.

They're just not going to do it. It's just not going to happen.[4]

David Kahneman, 2002 Nobel Prize in Economics, when asked about investors' long-term chances of beating a broad-based index fund

Kahneman won the Nobel Prize for his work on how natural human behaviors negatively affect investment decisions. Too many people, in his view, think they can find fund managers who can beat the market index over the long haul.

Any pension fund manager who doesn't have the vast majority—and I mean 70% or 80% of his or her portfolio—in passive investments [index funds] is guilty of malfeasance, nonfeasance, or some other kind of bad feasance! There's just no sense for most of them to have anything but a passive [indexed] investment policy.[5]

Merton Miller, 1990 Nobel Prize in Economics

Pension fund managers are trusted to invest billions of dollars for governments and corporations. In the U.S., more than half of them use indexed approaches. Those who don't, are, according to Miller, setting an irresponsible policy.

I have a global index fund with all-in expenses at eight basis points.[6]

Robert Merton, 1997 Nobel Prize in Economics

In 1994, Merton, a University Professor Emeritus at Harvard Business School, probably thought he could beat the market. After all, he was a director of Long Term Capital Management, a U.S. hedge fund (a type of mutual fund I will explain in Chapter 8) that reportedly earned 40 percent annual returns from 1994 to 1998. That was before the fund imploded, losing most of its shareholders' money, and shutting down in 2000.[7]

Naturally, a Nobel Prize winner such as Merton is a brilliant man—and he's brilliant enough to learn from his mistakes. When asked to share his investment holdings in an interview with PBS News Hour in 2009, the first thing out of Merton's mouth was the global index fund that he owns, which charges just eight basis points.[7] That's just a fancy way of saying that the hidden annual fee for his index is 0.08 percent. The average retail investor working with a financial adviser pays between 12 to 30 times more than that in fees. These fees can cost hundreds of thousands of dollars over an investment lifetime. I'll show you how to get your invest-ment fees down very close to what Robert Merton pays, learning from his mistakes.

More often (alas) the conclusions (supporting active manage-ment) can only be justified by assuming that the laws of arith-metic have been suspended for the convenience of those who choose to pursue careers as active managers.[8]

William F. Sharpe, 1990 Nobel Prize in Economics

If you were lucky enough to have Sharpe living across the street, he would tell you that he's a huge proponent of index funds and suggest that financial advisers and mutual fund manag-ers who pursue other forms of stock market investing are deluding themselves.[9]

If a financial adviser tries telling you not to invest in index funds, they're essentially suggesting that they're smarter than Warren Buffett and better with money than a Nobel Prize Laureate in Economics. What do you think?

What Causes Experts to Shake Their Heads

Advisers get paid well when you buy actively managed mutual funds (or unit trusts, as they're known outside of North America) so they love buying them for their clients' accounts. Advisers rarely get paid anything (if at all) when you buy stock market indexes, and desperately try to steer their clients in another (more profit-able) direction.

An actively managed mutual fund works like this:

1. Your adviser takes your money and sends it to a fund company.

2. That fund company combines your money with those of other investors into an active mutual fund.

3. The fund company has a fund manager who buys and sells stocks within that fund hoping that their buying and selling will result in profits for investors.

While a total U.S. stock market index owns nearly all the stocks in the U.S. market all of the time, an active mutual fund manager buys and sells selected stocks repeatedly.

For example, an active mutual fund manager might buy Coca-Cola Company shares today, sell Microsoft shares tomorrow, buy the stock back next week, and buy and sell General Electric Company shares two or three times within a 12-month period.

It sounds beneficially strategic, but academic evidence suggests that, statistically, buying an actively managed mutual fund is a loser's game when comparing it with buying index funds. Despite the strategic buying and selling of stocks by a fund manager for his or her fund, the vast majority of actively managed mutual funds will lose to the indexes over the long term. Here's why:

When the U.S. stock market moves up by, say, eight percent in a given year, it means the average dollar invested in the stock market increased by eight percent that year.[10] When the U.S. stock market drops by, say, eight percent in a given year, it means the average dollar invested in the stock market dropped in value by eight percent that year.

But does it mean that if the stock market made (hypothetically speaking) eight percent last year, every investor in U.S. stocks made an eight percent return on their investments that year? Of course not. Some made more, some made less. In a year where the markets made eight percent, half of the money that was invested in the market that year would have made more than eight percent and half of the money invested in the markets would have made less than eight percent. When averaging all the "successes" and "losses" (in terms of individual stocks moving up or down that year) the average return would have been eight percent.

Most of the money that's in the stock market comes from mutual funds (and index funds), pension funds, and endowment money.

So if the markets made eight percent this year, what do you think the average mutual fund, pension fund, and college endowment fund would have made on their stock market assets during that year?

The answer, of course, is going to be very close to eight percent. Before fees.

We know that a broad-based index fund would have made roughly eight percent during this hypothetical year because it would own every stock in the market—giving it the "average" return of the market. There's no mathematical possibility that a total stock market index can ever beat the return of the stock market. If the stock market makes 25 percent in a given year, a total stock market index fund would make about 24.8 percent after factoring in the small cost (about 0.2 percent) of running the index. If the stock market made 13 percent the following year, a total stock market index would make about 12.8 percent.

A financial adviser selling mutual funds seems, at first glance, to have a high prospect of getting his or her hand on your wallet right now. He or she might suggest that earning the same return that the stock market makes (and not more) would represent an "average" return—and that he or she could beat the average return through purchasing superior actively managed mutual funds.

If actively managed mutual funds didn't cost money to run, and if advisers worked for free, investors' odds of finding funds that would beat the broad-based index would be close to 50-50. In a 15-year-long U.S. study published in the *Journal of Portfolio Management*, actively managed stock market mutual funds were compared with the Standard & Poor's 500 stock market index. The study concluded that 96 percent of actively managed mutual funds underperformed the U.S. market index after fees, taxes, and survivorship bias.[11]

What's a survivorship bias?

When a mutual fund performs terribly, it doesn't typically attract new investors and many of its current customers flee the fund for healthier pastures. Often, the poorly performing fund is merged with another fund or it is shut down.

In November 2009, I underwent bone-cancer surgery—where large pieces of three of my ribs were removed, as well as chunks of my spinal process. But you want to know something? My five-year survivorship odds might be better than that of the average mutual fund. Examining two decades of actively managed mutual fund data, investment researchers Robert Arnott, Andrew Berkin, and Jia Ye tracked 195 actively managed funds, before reporting that the funds had a 17% mortality rate. According to the article they published with the *Journal of Portfolio Management* in 2000 called "How Well Have Taxable Investors Been Served in the 1980s and 1990s?" 33 of the 195 funds they tracked disappeared between 1979 and 1999.[12] No one can predict which funds are going to survive and which won't. The odds of picking an actively managed fund that you think will survive are no better than predicting which bone-cancer survivor will last the longest.

When the Best Funds Turn Malignant

You might think that the very best funds (those with long established track records) are large enough and strong enough to have a predictable longevity. They can't suddenly turn sour and disappear, can they?

That's what investors in the 44 Wall Street Fund thought. It was the top-ranked fund of the 1970s—outperforming every diversified fund in the industry and beating the S&P 500 index for 11 years in a row. Its success was temporary, however, and it went from being the best-performing fund in one decade to being the worst-performing fund in the next, losing 73 percent of its value in the 1980s. Consequently, its brand name was mud, so it was merged into the Cumberland Growth Fund in 1993, which then was merged into the Matterhorn Growth Fund in 1996. Today, it's as if it never existed.[13]

Then there was the Lindner Large-Cap Fund, another stellar performer that attracted a huge following of investors as it beat the S&P 500 index for each of the 11 years from 1974 to 1984. But you won't find it today. Over the next 18 years (from 1984 to 2002) it made its investors just 4.1% annually, compared with the 12.6% annual gain for investors in the S&P 500 index. Finally, the dismal track record of the Lindner Large-Cap Fund was erased when it was merged into the Hennessy Total Return Fund.[14]

You can read countless books on index-performance track records versus actively managed funds. Most say index funds have the advantage over 80 percent of actively managed funds over a period of 10 years or more. But they don't typically account for survivorship bias (or taxes, which I'll discuss later in this chapter) when making the comparisons. Doing so gives index funds an even larger advantage.

When accounting for fees, survivorship bias, and taxes, most actively managed mutual funds dramatically underperform index funds. In taxable accounts, the average U.S. actively managed fund underperformed the U.S. Standard & Poor's 500 stock market index by 4.8 percent annually from 1984 to 1999.[15]

Holes in the hulls of actively managed mutual funds

There are five factors dragging down the returns of actively managed U.S. mutual funds: expense ratios, 12B1 fees, trading costs, sales commissions, and taxes. Many people ask me why they don't see these fee liabilities mentioned on their mutual fund statements. With the possible exception of expense ratios and sales commissions—in very small print—the rest are hidden from view. Buying these products over an investment lifetime can be like entering a swimming race while towing a hunk of carpet through the water.

1. Expense Ratios

Expense ratios are costs associated with running a mutual fund. You might not realize this, but if you buy an actively managed mutual fund, hidden fees pay the salaries of the analysts and/or traders to choose which stocks to buy and sell. These folks are some of the highest paid professionals in the world; as such, they are expensive to employ. There's also the cost of maintaining their computers, paying office leases, ordering the paper they shuffle, using electricity, and compensating the advisers/salespeople for recommending their funds.

Then there are the owners of the fund company. They receive profits based on the costs skimmed from mutual fund expense ratios. I'm not referring to the average Joe who buys fund units in the mutual fund. I'm referring to the fund company's owners.

A fund holding a collective $30 billion would cost its investors (the average Joe) about $450 million every year (or 1.5 percent of its total assets) in expense-ratio fees. That money is sifted out of the mutual fund's value, but it isn't itemized for investors to see.[16] And the cash comes out whether the mutual fund makes money or not.

2. 12B1 Fees

Not every actively managed fund company charges 12B1 fees, but roughly 60 percent in the U.S. do. They can cost up to 0.25 percent, or a further $75 million a year for a $30 billion fund. These pay for marketing expenses including magazine, newspaper, television, and online advertising that's meant to lure new investors. That money has to come from somewhere. So current investors pay for new investors to join the party.[17] It's like a masked phantom pulling money from the wallets of mutual fund investors every night. Financial advisory statements don't itemize these expenses either.

3. Trading Costs

A third fee includes the fund's trading costs, which fluctuate year to year, based on how much buying and selling the fund managers do. Remember, actively managed mutual funds have traders at the helm who buy and sell stocks within the fund to try and gain an edge. But on average, according to the global research company Lipper, the average actively managed stock market mutual fund accrues trading costs of 0.2 percent annually, or $60 million a year on a $30 billion fund.[18] The costs of trading, 12B1 fees, and expense ratios aren't the only invisible albatrosses around the necks of mutual fund investors.

4. Sales Commissions

If the three hidden fees above are bringing you back in time to the nightmarish bottom of an elementary school dog pile, I have worse news for you. Many fund companies charge load fees: either a percentage up front to buy the fund (which goes directly to the salesperson) or a fee to sell the fund (which also goes directly to the salesperson). These fees can be as high as six percent. Many financial advisers love selling "loaded funds," which add a pretty nice kick to their own personal accounts but they aren't such a great deal for investors. A fund charging a sales fee of 5.75 percent, for example, has to gain 6.1 percent the following year just to break even on the deposited money. That might sound like strange math at first, but if you lose a given percentage to fees, you have to gain back a higher percentage to get your head back above water. For example, losing 50 percent in one year (turning $100 into $50) ensures that you will need to double your money the following year to get back to the original $100. Advisers choosing loaded funds for their clients put a whole new spin on "Piggy Bank," don't you think?

5. Taxes

More than 60 percent of the money in U.S. mutual funds is in taxable accounts.[19] This means when an actively managed mutual fund makes money in a given year, the investor has to pay taxes on that gain if the fund is held in a taxable account. There's a reason for that. Actively managed stock market mutual funds have fund managers who buy and sell stocks within their funds. If the stocks they sell generate an overall profit for the fund, then the investors in that fund (if they hold the fund in a taxable account) get handed a tax bill at the end of the year for the realized capital gain. The more trading a fund manager does, the less tax efficient the fund is.

In the case of a total stock market index fund, there's virtually no trading. The gains that are made on the stocks held don't generate a taxable hit for the funds' investors unless the investor sells the fund at a higher price than he or she paid. Rather than paying a high rate of capital gains tax every year, the index investor is able to defer his or her gains, paying them when he or she eventually sells the fund. Doing so allows for significantly higher compounding profits.

Mutual fund managers know that few people are going to compare their "after-tax" results with other mutual funds. For example, a fund making 11 percent a year might end up beating a fund making 12% a year—after taxes.[20] What makes one fund less tax efficient than another? It's the frequency of their buying and selling. The average actively managed mutual fund trades every stock it has during an average year. This is called a "100 percent turnover."[21] The trading practices of most mutual fund managers trigger short-term capital gains to the owners of those funds (when the funds make money). In the U.S., the short-term capital gain tax is a hefty penalty, but few actively managed fund managers seem to care.

In comparison, index-fund investors pay far fewer taxes in taxable accounts because index funds follow a "buy and hold" strategy. The more trading that occurs within a mutual fund, the higher the taxes incurred by the investor.

In the Bogle Financial Markets Research Center's 15-year study on after-tax mutual fund performances (from 1994 to 2009), it found actively managed stock market mutual funds were dramatically less tax efficient than a stock market index. For example, if you had invested in a fund (for your taxable account) that equaled the performance of the stock market index from 1994 to 2009, you would have paradoxically made less money than if you had invested in an index fund. But why would you have made less money if your fund had matched the performance of the stock index?

Before taxes, if your fund matched the performance of the U.S. index, you would have averaged 6.7 percent per year. After taxes though, for the actively managed fund to make as much money as a U.S. index fund, it would have needed to beat the index by a total of 16.2 percent over the 15-year period. This is assuming that the mutual fund manager bought and sold stocks with a regularity that equaled the average actively managed fund "turnover." A post-tax comparison of a mutual fund's performance against the performance of a stock market index isn't something that you will likely see on a typical mutual fund statement.[22] But in a taxable account, the post-tax gain is the only number that should count.

Adding high expense ratios, 12B1 fees, trading costs, sales commissions, and taxes to your investment is a bit like a boxer standing blindfolded in a ring and asking his opponent to hit him five times on the jaw before the opening bell. It's tough to put up a fair fight when you're already bleeding.

Figure 3.1   Dilbert's Take on Mutual Funds
Source: Dilbert Comics[23]

Figure 3.1 illustrates that if you learned this in school, it's likely that you would never consider investing in actively managed funds as an adult.

The futility of picking top mutual funds

You've just told your financial adviser that you'd like to invest in index funds—and now she's desperate. She won't make money (or not much) if you invest in indexes. It's far more lucrative for advisers to sell actively managed mutual funds instead. She needs you to buy the products for which she will be compensated handsomely, so here's the card she plays:

"Look, I'm a professional. And our company has access to researchers who will help me choose actively managed funds that will beat the indexes. Just look at these top-rated funds. I can show you dozens of them that have beaten the stock market index over the past 10 years. Of course I would only buy you top-rated funds."

Are there dozens of funds that have beaten the stock market indexes over the past 5, 10 or 15 years? Sure there are. But those funds, despite their track records, aren't likely to repeat their winning streaks. Mutual fund investing is a rare example of how, paradoxically, historical excellence means nothing.

Reality Check

Morningstar <www.morningstar.com> is an investment-research firm in the U.S. that awards funds based on a five-star system: five stars for a fund with a remarkable track record, all the way down to one star for a fund with a poor track record. Five-star funds tend to be those that have beaten the indexes over the previous five or ten years.

The problem is that fund rankings change all the time, and so do fund performances. Just because a fund has a five-star rating today doesn't mean that it will outperform the index over the next year, five years, or ten years. It's easy to look back in time and see great performing funds, but trying to pick them based on their historical performance is an expensive game.

Academics refer to something they call "reversion to the mean." In practical terms, actively managed funds that outperform the indexes typically revert to the mean or worse. In other words, buying the top historically performing funds can end up being the kiss of death.

If an adviser had decided to purchase Morningstar's five-star rated funds for you in 1994, and if he sold them as the funds slipped in the rankings (replacing them with the newly selected five-star funds), how do you think the investor would have performed from 1994 to 2004 compared with a broad-based U.S. stock market index fund?

Thanks to *Hulbert's Financial Digest,* an investment newsletter that rates the performance predictions of other newsletters, we have the answer which is emphasized in Figure 3.2.

One hundred dollars invested and continually adjusted to only hold the highest rated Morningstar funds from 1994 to 2004 would have turned into roughly $194, averaging 6.9 percent annually.

One hundred dollars invested in a broad-based U.S. stock market index from 1994 to 2004 would have turned into roughly $283, averaging 11 percent annually.[24]

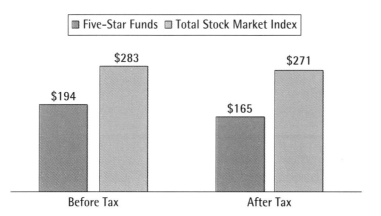

Figure 3.2   Five-Star Funds vs. Total Stock Market Index (1994–2004)
Source: John C. Bogle, *The Little Book of Common Sense Investing*

If you add further taxable liabilities, the results for the Morningstar superfunds would look even worse. You might as well be running with a monkey on your back.

One hundred dollars invested and continually adjusted to only hold the highest rated Morningstar funds from 1994 to 2004 would have turned into roughly $165 after taxes, at 5.15 percent annually.

One hundred dollars invested in a broad-based U.S. stock market index from 1994 to 2004 would have turned into roughly $271 after taxes, at 10.5 percent annually.

Interestingly, more than 98 percent of invested mutual fund money gets pushed into Morningstar's top-rated funds[25]

But choosing which actively managed mutual fund will perform well in the future is, in Burton Malkiel's words: "...like an obstacle course through hell's kitchen."[26] Malkiel, a professor of economics at Princeton University and the bestselling author of *A Random Walk Guide to Investing*, adds:

There is no way to choose the best [actively managed mutual fund] managers in advance. I have calculated the results of employing strategies of buying the funds with the best recent-year performance, best recent two-year performance, best five-year and ten-year performance, and not one of these strategies produced above average returns. I calculated the returns from buying the best funds selected by Forbes magazine ... and found that these funds subsequently produced below average returns.[27]

Still, most financial advisers won't give up. Their livelihood depends on you believing that they can do it, that they can find funds that will beat the market indexes.

Before we were married, my wife Pele was being "helped" by the U.S.-based financial service company Raymond James. <www.raymondjames.com/personal_investing/> She was sold actively managed mutual funds, and on top of the standard, hidden mutual fund fees, she was charged an additional 1.75 percent of her account value every year. An ongoing annual fee such as this—called a wrap fee, adviser fee, or account fee—is like a package of arsenic-laced cookies sold at your local health food store. Why did her adviser charge her this extra fee? Let's just say the adviser was servicing my wife the way the infamous Jesse James used to service train passengers—by taking the money and running. According to a 2007 article published in the U.S. weekly industry newspaper *Investment News,* Raymond James representatives are rewarded more for generating higher fees:

> *In the style of a 401(k) plan, the new deferred-compensation program this year gives a bonus of 1% to affiliated [Raymond James] reps who produce $450,000 in fees and commissions, a 2% bonus for $750,000 producers, and 3% for reps and advisers who produce $1 million. After that, the bonus, which will affect about 500 of the firm's 3,600 reps, increases one percentage point for every additional $500,000 in production, topping out at 10% for reps who produce $3.5 million in fees and commissions. That pushes those elite reps' payout to 100%—or even more—of their production, according to the company.[28]*

With pilfering incentives like these, salespeople and advisers make out like sultans.

Looking at my wife's investment portfolio in 2004, after tracking her account's performance, I calculated that her $200,000 account would have been $20,000 better off if she had been with an index fund over the previous five years, instead of with her adviser's actively managed mutual funds. In my calculation, I included the 1.75 percent annual "fleecing" fee her adviser charged, on top of the mutual funds' regular expenses.

When Pele asked her adviser about her account's relatively poor performance, he suggested some new mutual funds. When Pele asked about index funds, he dismissed the idea. Perhaps he had his eye on a big prize: a Porsche or an Audi convertible. He couldn't afford either if he bought his client index funds. So he switched her into a group of different actively managed funds that had beaten the indexes over the previous five years—all had Morningstar five-star ratings.

And how did those new funds do from 2004 to 2007? Badly. Despite the strong track records of those funds, they performed poorly, relative to the market indexes, after he selected them for Pele's account. So Pele fired the guy, and I married Pele.

Over an investment lifetime, it's a virtual certainty that a portfolio of index funds will beat a portfolio of actively managed mutual funds, after all expenses. But over a one-, three-, or even a five-year period, there's always a chance that a person's actively managed funds will outperform the indexes.

At a seminar I gave in 2010, a man I'll call Charlie, after seeing the returns of an index-based portfolio, said: "My investment adviser has beaten those returns over the past five years."

That's possible, but the statistical realities are clear. Over his investment lifetime, the odds are that Charlie's account will fall far behind an indexed portfolio.

In July 1993, *The New York Times* decided to run a 20-year contest pitting high-profile financial advisers (and their mutual fund selections) against the returns of the S&P 500 stock market index.

Every three months, the newspaper would report the results, as if the money was invested in tax-free accounts. The advisers were allowed to switch their funds, at no cost, whenever they wished.

What started out as a great publicity coup for these high-profile moneymen quickly turned into what must have felt like a quarterly tarring and feathering. After just seven years, the S&P 500 index was like a Ferrari to the advisers' Hyundai Sonatas, as revealed in Figure 3.3.

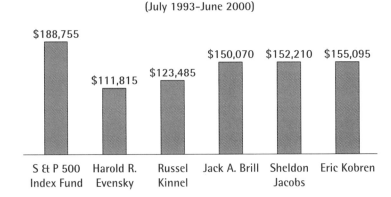

Fund Advisers Vs. S & P 500 Index
(July 1993–June 2000)

$188,755	$111,815	$123,485	$150,070	$152,210	$155,095
S & P 500 Index Fund	Harold R. Evensky	Russel Kinnel	Jack A. Brill	Sheldon Jacobs	Eric Kobren

Figure 3.3   *The New York Times* investment Contest

An initial $50,000 with the index fund in 1993 (compared with the following respective advisers' mutual fund selections) would have turned into the preceding sums by 2000.[29]

Mysteriously, after just seven years, *The New York Times* discontinued the contest. Perhaps the competitive advisers in the study grew tired of the humiliation.

Finding help without a conflict of interest

I'll liken the average financial adviser to chocolate cake. Can following a decadent nutritional plan of sugary baked goods make you feel good? Sure, for about 30 seconds as your taste buds relish the sticky sweetness. But the average financial adviser is as good for your long-term wealth as a chocolate cake diet is to your long-term health.

That said, there are financial advisers who charge by the hour for objective advice. While no one wants to add another bill to the y" financial planner charging an hourly rate can be a artnership that helps you create a successful portfo-nds.

:ans, there's an easy option. You can give your money vww.vanguard.com> a U.S.-based, nonprofit financial ny that happens to be the world's largest provider . You pay a small fee of $250 a year, and an adviser nguard will help you invest your money. When your account exceeds $250,000, the service is free.

AssetBuilder <www.assetbuilder.com> is another option. Based in Texas, this company charges low fees to operate as a broker that purchases index funds through a group called Dimensional Fund Advisors <www.dfaus.com/>. The small annual percentage fee for the service allows you to wipe your hands clean of managing your money yourself.

The following companies also charge low fees to build accounts of index funds for U.S. clients: RW Investments <www.rwin vestmentstrategies.com/background.html> (based in Maryland), Aperio Group <www.aperiogroup.com/> (based in California), and Evanson Asset Management <www.evansonasset.com/> (based in California).

There are other companies offering similar services. But be careful. Not all "fee-only" businesses offer low-fat services.

Where hidden calories lie

The number of fee-only, certified financial planners is increasing in the U.S. But you have to be careful. Fee-based adviser, Bert Whitehead, says in his book, *Why Smart People Do Stupid Things with Money*, that there are many organizations (such as American Express) that offer supposedly fee-based services, charging a small fee for a consultation, but they actually stuff investment accounts with their own brand of actively managed mutual funds and insurance products.[30] Actively managed mutual funds pad the coffers of investment service companies, so they are good for the businesses that sell you such products, but they're not good for you.

My hope, though, is that this book will give you every tool required to build portfolios of index funds yourself. Then you can hire a trustworthy accountant to provide advice on tax-sheltered accounts. Seeking an accountant's advice, you'll confidently avoid every conflict of interest corrupting the financial service industry—as long as your accountant doesn't sell financial products on the side.

For a review, however, let's take another look at total stock market index funds and actively managed mutual funds with a side-by-side comparison.

Table 3.1   Differences between Actively Managed Funds and Index Funds

Actively Managed Mutual Funds	Total Stock Market Index Fund
1. A fund manager buys and sells (trades) dozens or hundreds of stocks. The average fund has very few of the same stocks at the end of the year that it held at the beginning of the year.	1. A fund manager buys a large group of stocks—often more than a thousand. More than 96% of the stocks are the same from one year to the next. No "trading" occurs. Poor businesses that get dropped from the stock exchange get dropped from the index. New businesses get added.
2. The fund manager and his or her team conduct extensive research. Their high salaries compensate them for this service, adding to the cost of the fund. This added cost is paid by investors.	2. No research is done on individual stocks. A total market index fund can literally be run by a computer with no research costs. Its goal is to virtually own everything on the stock market so there are no "trading" decisions to make.

Table 3.1   (Cont'd)

Actively Managed Mutual Funds	Total Stock Market Index Fund
3. Stock trading (the buying and selling of stocks) within the fund generates commission expenses, which are taken out of the value of the mutual fund. The investors pay for these.	3. Because there's no "trading" involved, commissions for buying and/or selling are extremely low. The savings are passed down to investors.
4. Trading triggers tax consequences that are passed down to the investor when the fund is held in a taxable account. The taxman sends you a bill.	4. The lack of trading means that, even in a taxable account, capital gains can grow with minimal annual taxation. You keep the taxman at bay.
5. The fund manager focuses on certain stock sizes and sectors. For example, a small-cap fund would own small companies only; a large-cap fund would own large companies only; a value fund would own cheap companies only; a growth fund would own growth companies only.	5. A total stock market index would own stock in every category listed on the left—all wrapped up into one fund—because it owns "the entire stock market."
6. Companies offering mutual funds have owners who profit from the funds' fees. More fees raked from investors mean higher profits for the fund company's owners.	6. A fund company such as Vanguard is a "nonprofit" company. Vanguard is the world's largest provider of index funds, serving Americans, Australians, and the British. Low-cost indexes are also available to Asians, Canadians, and Europeans.
7. Because mutual fund companies have "owners" who seek profits for their fund company, there are aggressive sales campaigns and incentives paid to salespeople (advisers) to recommend their funds for clients. Investors pay for these.	7. Salespeople rarely tout indexes because they are less profitable for financial service companies to sell.
8. Actively managed fund companies pay annual "trailer fees" to advisers, rewarding them for selling their funds to investors—who end up paying for these.	8. Index funds rarely pay trailer fees to advisers.
9. Most U.S. fund companies charge sales or redemption fees—which go directly to the broker/adviser who sold you the fund. The investor pays for these.	9. Most index funds do not charge sales or redemption fees.
10. Actively managed mutual fund companies are extremely well liked by advisers and brokers.	10. Index funds are not well liked by most advisers and brokers.

Global citizens and index funds

If you're British or Australian, you can follow the lead with Vanguard, which has already set up shop in your country. As a nonprofit group, it might be the world's cheapest financial service operator, and indexing is their specialty.

If you're from another country, or if you're a global citizen working overseas, there are indexing options available for you as well (which I will discuss in Chapter 6). As high as U.S. actively managed stock mutual fund costs can run, the average non-U.S. fund is even more expensive. In a study presented in 2008 by *Oxford University Press*, Ajay Khorana, Henri Servaes, and Peter Tufano compared international fund costs, including estimated sales fees. According to the study, the country with the most expensive stock market mutual funds is Canada. Fortunately, for Canadians, Vanguard is planning to extend its services to its long-suffering northern neighbors.

High global investment costs make it even more important for global citizens outside of the U.S. to buy indexes for their investment accounts, rather than pay the heavy fees associated with actively managed mutual funds.

Table 3.2   The World's Actively Managed Stock Market Mutual Fund Fees

Country	Total Estimated Expenses, Including Sales Costs	Ranking of Least Expensive to Most Expensive Actively Managed Funds
Netherlands	0.82%	#1
Australia	1.41%	#2
Sweden	1.51%	#3
United States	1.53%	#4
Belgium	1.76%	#5
Denmark	1.85%	#6
France	1.88%	#7
Finland	1.91%	#8
Germany	1.97%	#9
Switzerland	2.03%	#10
Austria	2.26%	#11
United Kingdom	2.28%	#12
Dublin	2.40%	#13
Norway	2.43%	#14
Italy	2.44%	#15
Luxembourg	2.63%	#16
Spain	2.70%	#17
Canada	3.00%	#18

Source: "Mutual Fund Fees Around The World," *Oxford University Press*, 2008[31]

Who's Arguing against Indexes?

There are three types of people who argue that a portfolio of actively managed funds has a better chance of keeping pace with a diversified portfolio of indexes after taxes and fees over the long term.

Introduced first, dancing across the stage of improbability is your friendly neighborhood financial adviser. Pulling all kinds of tricks out of his bag, he needs to convince you that the world is flat, that the sun revolves around the Earth, and that he is better at predicting the future than a gypsy at a carnival. Mentioning index funds to him is like somebody sneezing on his birthday cake. He wants to eat that cake, and he wants a chunk of your cake too.

He exits, stage left, and a bigger hotshot strolls in front of the captive audience. Wearing a professionally pressed suit, she works for a financial advisory public relations department. Part of her job is to compose confusing market-summary commentaries that often accompany mutual fund statements. They read something like this:

> *Stocks fell this month because retail sales were off 2.5 percent, creating a surplus of gold buyers over denim, which will likely raise Chinese futures on the backs of the growing federal deficit, which caused two Wall Street Bankers to streak through Central Park because of the narrowing bond yield curve.*

Saying stock markets rose this year because more polar bears were able to find suitable mates before November has as much merit as the confusing economic drivel that financial planners write and distribute, assuming that nobody will read it anyway.

If you ask her, she will tell you that actively managed mutual funds are the way to go—but curiously doesn't mention she has killer mortgage payments on her $17 million, Hawaiian beachside summer home and you need to help her pay it.

Sadly, the third type of person who might tell you actively managed mutual funds have a better statistical long-term chance at profit (over indexes) are the prideful, or gullible folks who won't want to admit their advisers put their own financial interests above their clients.

Let's consider Peter Lynch, the man who was arguably one of history's greatest mutual fund managers. Before retiring at age 46, he managed the Fidelity Magellan fund <http://fundresearch.fidelity.com/mutual-funds/summary/316184100>, which captured public interest as it averaged 29 percent a year from 1977 to 1990.[32] More recently, however, Lynch's former fund has disappointed investors, earning a total of just 21 percent over the past decade, compared with 41 percent with the S&P 500 index.[33] Hammering the industry's faults, he says:

> *So it's getting worse, the deterioration by professionals is getting worse. The public would be better off in an index fund.*[34]

As the industry's idol from the 1980s, you might suggest that Lynch is a relic of a bygone era. Perhaps. But let's turn our attention to the present, and look at Bill Miller, the current actively managed fund manager of the Legg Mason Value Trust <www.leggmason.com> In 2006, *Fortune* magazine writer Andy Serwer called Miller "the greatest money manager of our time," after Miller's fund had beaten the S&P 500 index for the fifteenth straight year.[35] Yet, when *Money* magazine's Jason Zweig interviewed Miller in July 2007, Miller recommended index funds:

> *[A] significant portion of one's assets in equities should be comprised of index funds … Unless you are lucky, or extremely skillful in the selection of managers, you're going to have a much better experience going with the index fund.*[36]

Miller's quote was timely. Since 2007, his fund's performance has dramatically underperformed the total U.S. stock market index. Some mutual fund managers, of course (these are people who actually run the funds) are required by their employers to buy shares in the funds they run. But in taxable accounts, if fund managers don't have to commit their own money, they generally won't. Ted Aronson actively manages more than $7 billion for retirement portfolios, endowments, and corporate pension fund accounts. He's one of the best in the business. But what does he do with his own taxable money? As he told Jason Zweig, who was writing for *CNN Money* in 1999, all of his taxable money is invested with Vanguard's index funds:

*Once you throw in taxes, it just skewers the argument for
active [mutual fund] management ... indexing wins hands-
down. After tax, active management just can't win.[37]*

Or, in the words of a real heavy hitter, Arthur Levitt, former
chairman of the U.S. Securities and Exchange Commission:

*The deadliest sin of all is the high cost of owning some
mutual funds. What might seem to be low fees, expressed
in tenths of one percent, can easily cost an investor tens
of thousands of dollars over a lifetime.[38]*

You don't have to be disappointed with your investment results.
With disciplined savings and a willingness to invest regularly in low-
cost, tax-efficient index funds, you can feasibly invest half of what
your neighbors invest—over your lifetime—while still ending up
with more money.

You may not have learned these lessons in school, but they are
vital to your financial well being:

1. Index fund investing will provide the highest statistical
chance of success, compared with actively managed mutual
fund investing.

2. Nobody yet has devised a system of choosing which actively
managed mutual funds will consistently beat stock market
indexes. Ignore people who suggest otherwise.

3. Don't be impressed by the historical returns of any actively
managed mutual fund. Choosing to invest in a fund, based
on its past performance, is one of the silliest things an investor can do.

4. Index funds extend their superiority over actively managed
funds when the invested money is in a taxable account.

5. Remember the conflict of interest that most advisers
face. They don't want you to buy index funds because they
(the brokers) make far more money in commissions and
trailer fees when they convince you to buy actively managed funds.

Clearly avoiding the pitfall illustrated in Figure 3.4 will precipitate a far more promising future.

Figure 3.4   A Financial Adviser's Conflict of Interest
Source: Fang Yang

Notes

1. W. Gregory Guedel. "Ali versus Wilt Chamberlain—The Fight That Almost Was," *EastSideBoxing*, May 29, 2006, accessed October 20, 2010, http://www.eastsideboxing.com/news.php?p=7095&more=1http://www.eastsideboxing.com/news.php?p=7095&more=1.

2. Linda Grant, "Striking Out at Wall Street," *U.S. News & World Report,* June 20, 1994, 58.

3. Mel Lindauer, Michael LeBoeuf, and Taylor Larimore, *The Bogleheads Guide to Investing* (Hoboken, New Jersey: John Wiley & Sons, 2007), 83.

4. "Investors Can't Beat the Market, Scholar Says," *Orange County Register*, January 2, 2002, accessed October 30, 2010, http://www.ifa.com/Library/Support/Articles/Popular/KahnemanInvestorscantbeatmarket.htm.

5. Peter Tanous, "An Interview With Merton Miller," *Index Fund Advisors*, February 1, 1997, accessed October 30, 2010, http://www.ifa.com/Articles/An_Interview_with_Merton_Miller.aspx.

6. "Where Nobel Economists Put Their Money," accessed October 30, 2010, http://video.google.com/videoplay?docid= 9128160907104616152#.

7. Ibid.

8. "Arithmetic of Active Management," *Financial Analysts' Journal*, 47, No. 1, January/February 1991, 7.

9. Ibid.

10. John C. Bogle, *The Little Book of Common Sense Investing* (Hoboken, New Jersey: John Wiley & Sons, 2007), xiv.

11. David F. Swensen, *Unconventional Success, a Fundamental Approach to Personal Investment* (New York: Free Press, 2005), 217.

12. Robert D. Arnott, Andrew L. Berkin, and Jia Ye, "How Well Have Taxable Investors Been Served in the 1980s and 1990s?" *The Journal of Portfolio Management, Summer* 2000, Vol. 26, No. 4, 86.

13. Larry Swedroe, *The Quest For Alpha* (Hoboken, New Jersey: John Wiley & Sons, 2011), 13.

14. Larry Swedroe, *The Quest For Alpha,* 13–14.

15. David F. Swensen, *Unconventional Success, a Fundamental Approach to Personal Investment,* 217.

16. Ibid., 266.

17. Ibid.

18. John C. Bogle, *Common Sense on Mutual Funds* (Hoboken, New Jersey: John Wiley & Sons, 2010), 376.

19. Ibid., 384.

20. John C. Bogle, *The Little Book of Common Sense Investing,* 61.

21. John C. Bogle, *Common Sense on Mutual Funds,* 376.

22. Ibid.

23. Dilbert Comics, Reprinted with permission, Order Receipt #1591582.

24. John C. Bogle, *The Little Book of Common Sense Investing,* 90.

25. John C. Bogle, *Don't Count On It!* (Hoboken, New Jersey: John Wiley & Sons, 2011), 382.

26. Burton Malkiel, *The Random Walk Guide to Investing* (New York: Norton, 2003), 130.

27. Ibid.

28. Bruce Kelly, "Raymond James Unit Gives Bonuses to Big Producers," *Investment News—The Leading Source for Financial Advisors,* June 18, 2007.

29. Carole Gould, "Mutual Funds Report; A Seven-Year Lesson in Investing: Expect the Unexpected, and More," *The New York Times,* July 9, 2000, accessed April 15, 2011, http://www.nytimes

.com/2000/07/09/business/mutual-funds-report-seven-year-lesson-investing-expect-unexpected-more.html?.

30. Bert Whitehead, *Why Smart People Do Stupid Things With Money* (New York: Sterling Publishing, 2009), 205.

31. Ajay Khorana, Henri Servaes, and Peter Tufano, "Mutual Fund Fees Around the World," *The Review of Financial Studies 2008,* Vol. 22, No. 3 (Oxford University Press), accessed April 15, 2011, http://faculty.london.edu/hservaes/rfs2009.pdf.

32. "The Greatest Investors: Peter Lynch," *Investopedia*, accessed April 15, 2011, http://www.investopedia.com/university/greatest/peterlynch.asp.

33. Morningstar.com.

34. John C. Bogle, *The Little Book of Common Sense Investing,* 47–48.

35. Andy Serwer, "The Greatest Money Manager of Our Time," *Fortune,* November 15, 2006, accessed: April 15, 2011, http://money.cnn.com/2006/11/14/magazines/fortune/Bill_miller.fortune/index.htm.

36. Jason Zweig, "What's Luck Got to Do with It?" *Money*, July 18, 2007, accessed April 15, 2011, http://money.cnn.com/2007/07/17/pf/miller_interview_full.moneymag/.

37. Paul B. Farrell, "'Laziest Portfolio' 2004 Winner Ted Aronson Scores Repeat Win with 15 percent Returns," CBS Marketwatch.com, January 11, 2005, accessed April 15, 2011, http://www.marketwatch.com/story/results-are-in-and-laziest-portfolio-winner-is.

38. Mel Lindauer, Michael LeBoeuf, and Taylor Larimore, *The Bogleheads Guide to Investing,* 118.

RULE 4

Conquer the Enemy
in the Mirror

My brother Ian is a huge fan of the 1999 movie *Fight Club*, particularly the scene where the lead character Tyler, played by Edward Norton, is shown throwing haymaker punches at his own swollen face. Norton's character is metaphorically battling his materialistic urges. Most investors fight similar battles in a war against themselves.

Much of that internal grappling comes from misunderstanding the stock market. I can't promise to collar your inner doppelganger, but when you understand how the stock market works—and how human emotions can sabotage the best-laid plans—you'll experience greater investment success.

When a 10 Percent Gain Isn't
a 10 Percent Gain

Imagine a mutual fund that has averaged 10 percent a year over the past 20 years after all fees and expenses. Some years it might have lost money; other years it might have profited beyond expectation. It's a roller coaster ride, right? But imagine, on average, that it gained 10 percent annually even after the bumps, rises, twists, and turns. If you found a thousand investors who had invested in that fund from 1990 to 2010, you would expect that each would have netted a 10 percent annual return.

On average, however, they wouldn't have made anything close to that. When the fund had a couple of bad years, most investors react by putting less money in the fund or stop contributing to it entirely. Many investment advisers would say: "This fund hasn't been doing well lately. Because we're looking after your best interests, we're going to move your money to another fund that is doing better at the moment." And when the fund had a great year, most individual investors and financial advisers scramble to put more money in the fund, like feral cats around a fat salmon.

This behavior is self-destructive. They sell or cease to buy after the fund becomes cheap, and they buy like lunatics when the fund becomes expensive. If there weren't so many people doing it, we would call it a "disorder" and name it after some dead Teutonic psychologist. This kind of investment behavior ensures that investors pay higher-than-average prices for their funds over time. Whether it's an index fund or an actively managed mutual fund, most investors perform worse than the funds they own—because they like to buy high, and they hate buying low. That's a pity.

John Bogle, the founder of Vanguard, explains in his book, *The Little Book of Common Sense Investing*, that the average mutual fund reported a 10 percent annual gain from 1980 to 2005 after fees and expenses, but investors in those funds over the same time period only averaged 7.3 percent per year.[1] Their fear of low prices prevented them from buying when the funds were low, while their elation at high prices encouraged purchases when fund prices were high. Such bizarre behavior has devastating financial consequences when investors give away 2.7 percent annually because of their knee-jerking alter egos.

Over a 25-year period, that's a pretty expensive habit:

$50,000 invested at 10 percent a year for 25 years = $541,735.29

$50,000 invested at 7.3 percent a year for 25 years = $291,046.95

Cost of irrationality = $250,688.34

But what if you didn't care what the stock market was doing?

As investors, you really don't have to watch the stock market to see if it's going up or down. In fact, if you bought a market index fund for 25 years, with an equal dollar amount going into that fund each month (called "dollar-cost averaging") and if that fund averaged 10 percent annually, you would have averaged 10 percent or more. Why more? If you put a regular $100 a month into a fund, that $100 would have bought fewer unit shares of that fund when prices were high, but it would have bought more unit shares of that fund when prices were lower.

Most investors don't do that—they exhibit nutty behavior

Combine the crazy behavior of the average investor with the fees associated with actively managed mutual funds, and the average investor ends up with a comparatively puny portfolio compared with the disciplined investor who puts in the same amount of money every month into index funds. Table 4.1 categorizes investors who will be working—and adding to their investments—for at least the next five years.

I'm not going to suggest that all indexed investors are evolved enough to ignore the market's fearful roller coaster, while shunning the self-sabotaging caused by fear and greed. But if you can learn to invest regularly in indexes and remain calm when the markets fly upward or downward, you'll grow far wealthier. In Table 4.2, you can see examples based on actual U.S. returns between 1980 and 2005.

The figure on the left side ($84,909.01) is probably a little generous. The 10 percent annual return for the average actively managed fund has been historically overstated because it doesn't include sales fees, adviser wrap fees, or the added liability of taxes in a taxable account.

Disciplined index investors who don't self-sabotage their accounts can end up with a portfolio that's easily twice as large as that of the average investor over a 25-year period.

Table 4.1   The Average Investor Compared with the Evolved Investor

The Average Investor	The Evolved Investor
Buys actively managed mutual funds.	Buys index funds.
Feels good about his or her fund when the price increases, so they buy more of it.	Buys equal dollar amounts of the indexes and knows, happily, that this buys fewer units as the stock market rises.
Feels badly about his or her fund when the price decreases, so the person limits purchases or sells the fund.	Loves to see the stock index fall in value. If he or she has the money, the person increases their purchases.

Table 4.2   Historical Differences Between the Average Investor and the Evolved Investor

The Average Investor	The Evolved Investor
$100 a month invested from 1980 to 2005 in the average U.S. mutual fund (roughly $3.33 a day). 10% annual average	$100 a month invested from 1980 to 2005 in the U.S. stock market index (roughly $3.33 a day). 12.3% annual average
Minus 2.7% annually for the average investor's self-sabotaging behavior.	No deficit for silly behavior.
25-year average annual return for investors: 7.3%	25-year average annual return for investors: 12.3%
Portfolio value after 25 years = $84,909.01	Portfolio value after 25 years = $198,181.90

Note: Although the U.S. stock market has averaged about 10 percent annually over the past 100 years, there are periods where it performs better and there are periods where it performs worse. From 1980 to 2005, the U.S. stock market averaged slightly more than 12.3 percent a year.[2]

Small details like these can allow people with middle-class incomes to amass wealth more effectively than their high-salaried neighbors—especially if the middle-class earners think twice about spending more than they can afford. Even if your neighbors invest twice as much as you each month, if they are average, they will buy actively managed mutual funds, and they will either chase hot-performing funds or fail to keep a regular commitment to their investments when the markets fall. They'll feel good about buying into the markets when they're expensive, and they won't be as keen to buy when they're on sale.

I don't want you to be like your neighbors. Avoid that kind of self-destructive behavior and you'll increase your odds of building wealth as an investor.

It's Not Timing the Market that Matters; It's Time in the Market

There are smart people (and people who aren't so smart) who mistakenly think they can jump in and out of the stock market at opportune moments. It seems simple. Get in before the market rises and get out before the market drops. This is referred to as "market timing." But most financial advisers have a better chance beating Roger Federer in a tennis match than effectively timing the market for your account.

Vanguard's Bogle, who was named by *Fortune* magazine as one of the four investment giants of the twentieth century has this to say about market timing:

> *After nearly 50 years in this business, I do not know of anybody who has done it successfully and consistently. I don't even know anybody who knows anybody who has done it successfully and consistently.*[3]

When the markets go raving mad, dramatically jumping in and out can be tempting. But stock markets are highly irrational and characterized by short-term swings. The stock market often will fly higher than most people expect during a euphoric phase, while plunging further than anticipated during times of economic duress. There's a simple, annual, mechanical strategy that you can follow to protect your money from excessive crashes, which I'll outline in Chapter 5. Your investment will still fall in value when the stock market falls, but not as much as your neighbor's— and that can help you sleep better when the stock market isn't cooperating.

The strategy that I'll show you doesn't involve trying to guess the stock market's direction. Forecasting where it's going to go over a short period is like trying to guess which frantic, nightly moth is going to get singed by the light bulb first.

Doing nothing but holding onto your total stock market index fund might sound boring during a financial boom and it might sound terrifying during a financial meltdown. But the vast majority of people (including professionals) who try jumping in and out of the stock market allow their emotional judgments to hurt their profits as they often end up buying high and selling low.

What can you miss by guessing wrong?

Studies show that most market moves are like the flu you got last year or like the mysterious $10 bill you found in the pocket of your jeans. In each case, you don't see it coming. Even when looking back at the stock market's biggest historical returns, Jeremy Siegel, a professor of business at University of Pennsylvania's Wharton School, suggests that there's no rhyme or reason when it comes to market activity. He looked back at the biggest stock market moves since 1885 (focusing on trading sessions where the markets moved by five percent or more in a single day) and tried connecting each of them to a world event.[4]

In most instances, he couldn't find logical explanations for such large stock market movements—and he had the luxury of looking back in time, and trying to match the market's behavior with historical world news. If a smart man like Siegel can't make connections between world events and the stock market movements with the benefit of hindsight, then how is someone supposed to predict future movements based on economic events—or the prediction of economic events to come? It's as improbable as guessing which directional changes a frantic, unleashed 10-month-old Labrador retriever is going to make in an open field.

If you're ever convinced to act on somebody's short-term stock market prediction, it could end up being a very expensive mistake. Let's look at the U.S. stock market over the period of January 1, 1982, to December 31, 2005, as an example.

During this time, the stock market averaged returns of 10.6 percent annually.

But if you didn't have money in the stock market during the best 10 trading days, your average return would have dropped to 8.1 percent annually. If you missed the best 50 trading days, your average return would have been just 1.8 percent annually.[5] Markets can move so unpredictably, and so quickly. If you take money out of the stock market for a day, a week, a month, or a year, you could miss the best trading days of the decade. You'll never see them coming. They just happen. More importantly, as I said before, neither you nor your broker are going to be able to predict them.

Legendary investor and self-made billionaire Kenneth Fisher, who has his own column in *Forbes* magazine, had this to say about market timing:

> *Never forget how fast a market moves. Your annual return can come from just a few big moves. Do you know which days those will be? I sure don't and I've been managing money for a third of a century.*[6]

The easiest way to build a responsible, diversified investment account is with stock and bond index funds. I'll discuss bond indexes in Chapter 5, but for now, just recognize them as instruments that generally create stability in a portfolio. Many people view them as boring because they don't produce the same kind of long-term returns that stocks do. But they don't fall like stocks are apt to do either. They're the steadier, slower, and more dependable part of an investment portfolio. A responsible portfolio has a certain percentage allocated to the stock market and a certain percentage allocated to the bond market, with an increasing emphasis on bonds as the investor ages.

But when stocks start racing upward and everyone's getting giddy on the profits they're making, most people ignore their bonds (if they own any at all) and they buy more stocks. Many financial advisers fall prey to the same weakness. But those ignoring their planned allocations between stocks and bonds set themselves up for disaster.

How can you ensure that you're never a victim? It's far easier than you might think. If you understand exactly what stocks are—and what you can expect from them—you'll fortify your odds of success.

On Stocks . . . What You Really Should Have Learned in School

The stock market is a collection of businesses. It isn't just a squiggly bunch of lines on a chart or quotes in the newspaper. When you own shares in a stock market index fund, you own something that's as real as the land you're standing on. You become an indirect owner of all kinds of industries and businesses via the companies you own within your index: land, buildings, brand names, machinery, transportation systems, and products, to name a few. Just understanding this key concept can give you a huge advantage as an investor.

Business earnings and stock price growth are two separate things, but long term, they tend to reflect the same result. For example, if a business grew its profits by 1,000 percent over a 30-year period, we could expect the stock price of that business to appreciate similarly over the same period.

It's the same for a stock market index. If the average company within an index grew by 1,000 percent over 30 years (that's 8.32 percent annually) we could expect the stock market index to perform similarly. Long term, stock markets predictably reflect the fortunes of the businesses within them. But over shorter periods, the stock market can be as irrational as a crazy dog on a leash. And it's the crazy dog's movements that can—if we let them—lure us closer to poverty than to wealth.

True stock market experts understand dogs on leashes

I used to have a dog named Sue who behaved like we were feeding her rocket fuel instead of dog food. If you turned your back on her in the backyard, she'd enact a scene from the U.S. television show *Prison Break*, bounding over the five-foot-high fence in our yard and straining diplomatic relations between our family and those whose gardens she would destroy.

When I took her for extended runs on wide, open fields, she was able to burn off some octane. I would run in a single direction while she darted upward, backward, right, then left. But collared by a very long rope, she couldn't escape.

If I ran from the lake to the barn with Sue on a leash, and if it took me 10 minutes to get there, then any observer would realize it would take the dog 10 minutes to get there as well. True, the dog could bolt ahead or lag behind while sticking its nose in a gift left behind by another canine. But ultimately, it can't cover the distance much slower or much faster than I do—because of the leash.

Now imagine a bunch of emotional gamblers who watch and bet money on leashed dogs. When a dog bursts ahead of its owner, the gamblers put money on the sprinting dog, betting that it will sprint far off into the distance. But the dog's on a leash, so it can't get too far ahead of its owner. When the leashed dog gets ahead, it's destined to either slow down or stop—so that the owner can catch up.

But the gamblers don't think about that. If they see the dog bounding along without noticing the leash, they place presumptuous bets that the dog will maintain its frenetic pace. Their greed wraps itself around their brains and squeezes. Without that cranial compression, they would see that the leashed dog couldn't outpace its owner.

It sounds so obvious, doesn't it? Now get this: the stock market is exactly like a dog on a leash. If the stock market races at twice the pace of business earnings for a few years, then it has to either wait for business earnings to catch up, or it will get choke-chained back in a hurry. But a rapidly rising stock market can cause people to forget that reality. I'll use an individual stock to prove the point.

Coca-Cola Bounds from Its Owner

From 1988 to 1998, the Coca-Cola Company <www.coca-cola.com> increased its profits as a business by 294 percent. During this short period (and yes, 10 years is a stock market blip) Coca-Cola's stock price increased by 966 percent. Because it was rising rapidly, investors (including mutual fund managers) fell over themselves to buy Coca-Cola shares, pushing the share price even higher. Greed might be the greatest hallucinogenic known to man.

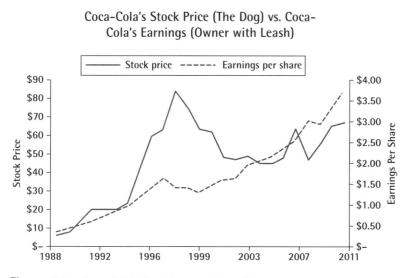

Coca-Cola's Stock Price (The Dog) vs. Coca-Cola's Earnings (Owner with Leash)

Figure 4.1   Coca-Cola's Stock Price vs. Coca-Cola's Earnings
Source: Value Line Investment Survey

The dog (Coca-Cola's stock price) was racing ahead of its master (Coca-Cola's business earnings). A rational share price increase must fall in line with profits, correct? If Coca-Cola's business earnings increased by 294 percent from 1988 to 1998, we would assume that its stock price would grow by a percentage that was at least somewhat similar, maybe a little higher and maybe a little lower. But Coca-Cola's stock price growth of 966 percent was irrational, compared with its business earnings increase of 294 percent.[7]

Can you see what happened to the blazing Coca-Cola share price in Figure 4.1 when it got far ahead of Coca-Cola's business profits?

The dog eventually dropped back to meet its owner. After blazing ahead at 29 percent a year for a decade (from 1988 to 1998) Coca-Cola's stock price eventually "heeled." It had to. You can see by the chart that the stock price was lower in 2011 than it was in 1998.

Coca-Cola's earnings growth and stock price were realigned, much like a leashed dog with its owner.

You can look at the earnings growth of any stock you choose. Over a long period, the stock's price might jump around, but it will never disconnect itself from the business earnings. To see a few examples for yourself, you can log on to *The Value Line Investment Survey* <http://www3.valueline.com/dow30/index.aspx?page=home>. The U.S. research company offers free, online historical data of the 30 Dow Jones Industrial stocks.

The Madness of People

Coca-Cola wasn't the only business with a share price that was out of step with its business earnings. Stock market investors worldwide euphorically flocked to stocks in the late 1990s, as they were motivated by ... rising prices. The stock buying grew more frenzied during the latter part of the decade as stock prices reached lofty new heights. The U.S. (for example) went through a period of strong economic growth during the 1990s, but the prices of stocks were rising twice as fast as the level of business earnings. It couldn't last forever, however. The decade that followed saw the racing, leashed dogs eventually fall back in line with their owners who were moving at a much slower rate.

Global stock markets also took a breather between the year 2000 and 2010, rising just 21 percent for the decade, after climbing 250 percent between 1989 and 1999, as measured by the MSCI index of developed country stock markets.[8]

Stocks Go Crazy Every Generation

Long term, whether we're talking about Coca-Cola or a stock market index, there's one reality: the growth of stock market prices will correlate themselves directly with the growth of the businesses they represent. It's supply and demand that pushes stock prices over the short term. If there are more buyers than sellers, the stock price (or the stock market index in general) will rise. If there are more sellers than buyers, stocks will drop. And when prices rise, people feel more confident about that investment. They buy more, pushing the price even higher. People become drunk on their own greed, not recognizing that bubbles form when price levels dramatically exceed business profit growth.

"History Doesn't Repeat Itself, But It Does Rhyme"—Mark Twain[9]

As far back as we have records, at least once every generation, the stock market goes bonkers. Table 4.3 shows three periods from the past 90 years showing the U.S. market as represented by the Dow Jones Industrial stocks. You can see, in each case, share price levels that grossly exceeded earnings levels, and the terrible returns that followed as the "dogs" were caught by their "owners."

Note from 1920 to 1929, the Dow stocks' average business growth amounted to 118 percent over the 10-year period. But the prices of the Dow stocks increased by 271.2 percent over that decade, so if someone invested in all 30 Dow stocks in 1920 and held them until 1929, they would have gained more than 271 percent not including dividends, and close to 300 percent including dividends. Because stock prices can't exceed business growth for long, the decade that followed (1930–1940) saw the stock market fall by an overall total of 40.9 percent. Again, the leashed dog can't escape its owner.

Table 4.3   Prices of Stocks Can't Outpace Business Earnings for Long

Years When Stock Prices Exceeded Business Earnings	Growth in Business Earnings (the Pace of the Dog's Owner)	Growth in Stock Prices (the Pace of the Dog)	Stock Price Decline (the Dog's Overall Progress) During the Following Decade
1920–1929	+118%	+271.2%	−40.9%
1955–1965	+50%	+98.5%	−9.3%
1990–2000	+152%	+290%	−0.17%

Note: Figures do not include dividends
Source: The Value Line Investment Survey[10]

The two other time periods during the past 90 years where investors lost sight of the connections between business earnings and stock price appreciation occurred from 1955 to 1965 and from 1990 to 2000. You can see the results in Table 4.3.

Anyone investing in a broad U.S. stock market index would have gained more than 300 percent (including dividends) in the 10 short years between 1990 and 2000. Did business earnings increase by 300 percent? Not even close. That's the main reason the markets stalled from 2000 to 2010.

How does this relate to you?

Every generation, it happens again. Stock prices go haywire, and when they do, many people abandon conservative investment strategies. The more rapidly the markets rise, the more reckless most investors become. They pile more and more money into stocks, ignoring their bonds. And when the markets eventually fall or stagnate, they curse their bad luck. But luck has little to do with it. The blame rests on investors' lack of discipline or their ignorance about the stock market.

Internet Madness and the Damage It Caused

The greatest Titanic period of delusion sailed during the technology stock mania of the late 1990s. The stocks that were riskiest were those companies with the greatest disconnection between their business earnings and their stock prices.

Many Internet-based businesses weren't even making profits but their stock prices were soaring, pushed upward by the media and the scintillating stories of Silicon Valley's super-rich. Most of their investors probably didn't know that there's a direct long-term connection between stock prices and business earnings. They probably didn't know that it's not realistic for businesses to grow their earnings by 150 percent a year—year after year, no matter what the business is. And if businesses can't grow earnings by 150 percent on an annual basis, then their stocks can't either.

Some of the more famous promoters at the time were such high-profile financial analysts as Morgan Stanley's Mary Meeker, Merrill Lynch's Henry Blodgett, and Solomon Smith Barney's Jack Grubman. But they might have a tough time showing their faces today. For all I know, the top Internet stock analysts of the 1990s are finding a safer, more peaceful existence in the jungles of Borneo. I can imagine a few people wanting their heads. Their media-thrown voices tossed buckets of gas on the flames of madness when technology-based companies without profits were priced in the stratosphere. Meeker, Blodgett, and Grubman were encouraging the average person to buy, buy, buy.

One difference between this period and the bubbles of previous generations was the speed that the bubble grew, thanks to the Internet as a rapid communication channel. One trans-generational similarity, however, was the investors' attitude that "this time it would be different." In each period where stock prices disconnect from earnings levels, you find people who think that history is going to rewrite itself, that stock prices no longer need to reflect earnings, and that leashed dogs everywhere can develop mutations, grow wings, and lead flocks of Canadian geese on their way to Florida. Long term, stock prices reflect business earnings. When they don't, it spells trouble.

Even shares of the world's largest technology companies sold at nosebleed prices as they defied business profit levels. And, as shown in Table 4.4, when cold, hard business earnings eventually yanked the price leashes back to Earth, people who had ignored the age-old premise (that business growth and stock growth is directly proportional) eventually lost their shirts. Investing $10,000 in a few of the new millennium's most popular stocks during 2000 would have resulted in some devastating losses for investors.

Table 4.4   How Investors were Punished

Formerly Hot Stocks	$10,000 Invested at the Market High in 2000	Value of the Same $10,000 at the Low of 2001–2002
Amazon.com	$10,000	$700
Cisco Systems	$10,000	$990
Corning Inc.	$10,000	$100
JDS Uniphase	$10,000	$50
Lucent Technologies	$10,000	$70
Nortel Networks	$10,000	$30
Priceline.com	$10,000	$60
Yahoo!	$10,000	$360

Source: Morningstar and Burton Malkiel, A Random Walk Down Wall Street, 2003[12]

The stories of wealth enticed individual investors and fund management firms alike before the eventual collapse of the dot-com bubble.

Mutual fund companies rushed to create technology-based funds that they could sell. The job of fund companies, of course, isn't to make money for you or me. Their primary job is to make money for their companies' owners or shareholders.

There's a saying that "Wall Street will sell what Wall Street can sell." In this case, newly introduced technology-stock mutual funds were first-class tickets on airplanes with near-empty fuel tanks. Passengers giggled with delight as they soared into the clouds . . . until the fuel ran out.

Sadly, there were plenty of regular middle-class folk who climbed aboard this soon-to-be-plunging craft. When the plane hurtled into the ground, many investors in technology funds and Internet stocks lost nearly everything they had invested.

Few players in the Internet stock fiasco escaped unscathed. You might imagine loads of people getting out on top, or near the top, but the hysterical era of easily quadrupling your money within a matter of months swept through amateur and professional investors alike. Nobody really knew where that "top" was going to be, so loads of people kept climbing into tech stocks.

I'd be lying if I claimed to avoid the tech sector's sirens. In 1999, I succumbed to buying shares in one of the technology stock darlings of the day, Nortel Networks <www.nortel.com/>.

It was silly of me to buy it, but watching my friends making bucket loads of easy money on Internet stocks while I sat on the sidelines was more than I could take. Swept up in the madness, it didn't matter that I didn't really know what the company did.

Eventually getting around to reading Nortel's annual report, I recognized that the company had been losing more and more money since 1996. But I didn't care. Sure, it made me nervous, but the stock price was rising and I didn't want to be left behind.

What was worse was that every year since 1996, the business was losing more and more money while its stock price was going in the opposite direction: up! I paid $83 a share. When that stock price rose to $118, I had made a 42 percent profit. Late getting onto the Nortel train, I couldn't believe the money I had made in such a short time. Recognizing a quick profit, I figured it would be wise to sell, which is exactly what I did at $118 a share. If only the story ended there. No sooner did I sell than the price rose to $124 a share.

Then I read an analyst's report suggesting that the share price was going to rise to $150 before the year was up. What was I doing, selling at $118?

Shortly after the stock price dipped to $120, and like a knucklehead, I bought back the shares I had previously sold. I was watching the dog, while ignoring the owner's *rigor mortis.*

And that's when gravity hurtled the stock price down to $100 a share . . . then $80 a share . . . then $50 a share. Suddenly, people were noticing the smell.

I sold at $48, losing almost half of what I put into my investment. I got burned for buying a stock I never should have bought in the first place because—despite the meteoric rise in its stock price—the business itself hadn't made a dime in years.

But I was lucky. Today, those same shares are worth pennies.

Many of my friends never sold. It's a shameful reminder on a brokerage statement of what can happen when we mix greed and ignorance.

Taking Advantage of Fear and Greed

Buying a total stock market index fund needn't be boring. If you can be greedy when others are fearful and fearful when others are greedy, you can add a touch of nitrate to your investment portfolio. You don't need to follow investment news or follow the markets. You just need to utilize the safest component of your investment portfolio—your bonds.

The disastrous events of September 11, 2001 invoked tremendous fear in the American people when terrorists hijacked two airliners and flew them into New York's World Trade Center. After the twin towers collapsed, the stock markets were temporarily closed. Sadly, nearly 3,000 people were killed in the terrorist attack.

But long term, how would that affect American business profits? As catastrophic as the event had been, it wasn't likely to have a permanent affect on the number of Coca-Cola cans sold worldwide, or McDonald's hamburger sales <www.mcdonalds.com/us/en/home.html>, or Starbucks coffee sales <www.starbucks.com>, or Safeway's food sales <www.safeway.com/IFL/Grocery/Home>. Americans are resilient, and so are their businesses.

But when the stock markets reopened after the terrorist attack, the prices of U.S. businesses dropped.

Short term, most investors prove their irrationality

Many investors don't think about the stock market as a representation of something real—like true business earnings. Fear and greed rule the short-term irrationality of stock markets. But thinking about the market as a group of businesses, and not a squiggly line on a chart or a quote in the paper, can fertilize your wealth. When there's a disconnection between business profits and stock prices, you can easily take advantage of the circumstances. What happened in the stock markets after 9/11 was the antithesis of the boom times of the late 1990s. Stock prices fell like football-sized chunks of hail, but business earnings were hardly affected.

When the New York Stock Exchange reopened after the 9/11 attacks, it might as well have held up a giant neon sign: "Stocks on sale today!" The U.S. stock market opened 20 percent lower than its opening level the previous month. Scraping together every penny I could muster, I dumped money into the stock market like a crazed shopper at a "going out of business" sale. Speculators hate doing that because they're continually worried the markets will fall further. Real investors never think like that. They care more about what the markets will be doing in 20 years not next week.

Worrying about the immediate future is letting the stock market lead you by the gonads.

Most people have a backward view of the markets

The Oracle of Omaha, Warren Buffett, laid out a quiz in his 1997 letter to Berkshire Hathaway <www.berkshirehathaway.com> shareholders. If you can honestly pass this quiz, you'll be on your way to doing well in the stock market. But most investors and most financial advisers would fail this little quiz, and that's one of the reasons most people are poor investors. As Buffett wrote:

> *If you plan to eat hamburgers throughout your life and are not a cattle producer, should you wish for higher or lower prices for beef? Likewise, if you are going to buy a car from time to time but are not an auto manufacturer, should you prefer higher or lower car prices? These questions, of course, answer themselves.*
>
> *But now for the final exam: If you expect to be a net saver during the next five years, should you hope for a higher or lower stock market during that period?*
>
> *Many investors get this one wrong. Even though they are going to be net buyers of stocks for many years to come, they are elated when stock prices rise and depressed when they fall. In effect, they rejoice because prices have risen for the 'hamburgers' they will soon be buying.*
>
> *This reaction makes no sense. Only those who will be sellers of equities [stock market investments] in the near future should be happy at seeing stocks rise. Prospective purchasers should much prefer sinking prices.[12]*

Think of the stock market as a grocery store filled with nonperishable items. When prices fall, it's a good idea to stock up on those products because the prices will inevitably rise again. If you like to buy canned beans and the store is selling them this week at a 20 percent discount, you have a choice. You can sit on your haunches and wonder whether they'll be even cheaper the following week, or you can stop being silly and just buy the beans. If the price drops further the following month, you can always buy more cans. But if you sit on your butt and miss out on the sale (because you're speculating that beans will get cheaper), well ... you miss out on the sale.

A stock market drop is the same as a sale at your local supermarket. I'll show you how to take advantage of such opportunities.

Opportunities after Chaos

Where did I get the money to take advantage of the stock market's discounted level when the markets reopened after 9/11? I sold some of my bonds. It didn't take any kind of special judgment on my part. I just stuck to a mechanical strategy, which I'll explain further in Chapter 5.

Unfortunately, the money I invested in the U.S. stock market index in September 2001 went on to gain 15 percent over just a few months. By January 2011 (even after the financial crisis of 2008–2009), the value of my stock purchases in the autumn of 2001 was up more than 55 percent, including dividends. But that upset me. Yes, you read that right. I was upset to see my stock market investments rise.

After 9/11, I wanted the markets to stay down. I was hoping to keep buying into the stock markets for many years at a discounted rate. It's a bit like betting that a sleeping dog on a long leash is eventually going to have to get up and run to catch its sprinting owner. The longer the leash and the longer that dog sleeps, the more money I can put on the dog, which will eventually tear after its owner up the hill, pulling my wheelbarrow load of money behind it. Sadly for me, the stock market didn't sleep in its discounted state for long.

Of course, not everybody is going to be happy about a sinking or stagnating stock market. My apologies to retirees. If you're retired, there's no way you're going to want to see plummeting stock prices. You're no longer able to buy cheap stocks when you're not making a salary. And, you'll be regularly selling small pieces of your investments every year to cover living expenses.

Younger people who will be adding to their portfolios for at least five years or more need to celebrate when markets fall. I didn't think I would get another opportunity to benefit from irrational fear after September 2001. A plunging stock market is a

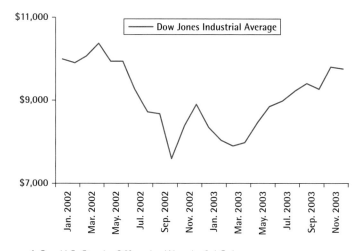

Figure 4.2   U.S. Stocks Offered a Wonderful Sale
Source: Yahoo! Finance historical price tables for Dow Jones Industrials

special treat for a wage earner—one that doesn't come along every day. But another opportunity fell on my lap again between 2002 and 2003, (as shown in Figure 4.2) with the stock market eventually selling at a 40 percent discount from its 2001 high, after the U.S. announced it was going to war with Iraq.

Was the average U.S. business going to make 40 percent less money? Were businesses like PepsiCo <www.pepsico.com>, Wal-Mart <www.walmart.com>, Exxon Mobil <www.exxonmobil.com/Corporate>, and Microsoft <www.microsoft.com/en-us/default.aspx> going to see a 40 percent drop in profits? Even at the time, it would have been really tough to find anyone who believed that. Yet U.S. businesses were trading at a 40 percent discount on the stock market. I was salivating, and hoping that the markets would stay down this time—for years if possible. I wanted to load up.

I didn't know how low the markets would fall, so I wasn't lucky enough to buy stock indexes at the very bottom of the market's plunge. But it didn't matter to me. Once the "20 percent off" flags were waving in my face, I was a chocoholic stowaway in Willy Wonka's factory. The stock market continued to fall as I continued to buy. If I could have taken an extra job to give me more money to take advantage of cheap stock prices, I probably would have done it. For some reason, most investors were doing what they typically do: They overreact when prices fall, sending stocks to mouthwatering levels, by selling when they should be buying. They become afraid of a discounted sale, hoping (and yes, this is a true representation of insanity) that they can soon pay higher prices for their stock market products. They miss the point of what stocks are. Stocks represent ownership in real businesses.

Again, I hoped that the stock markets would keep falling in 2003, or that they would stay low for a few years so I could gorge at the buffet.

It was not to be. I was disappointed as the U.S. stock market index began a long recovery from 2002–2003 until the end of 2007, rising more than 100 percent from its low point in just four years. Retirees would have been celebrating, but I was crying in my oatmeal. The big supermarket sale was over.

As the stock market roared ahead in 2007, I didn't put a penny in my stock indexes. I bought bond indexes instead. Following a general rule of thumb, I wanted my bond allocation to equal my age. For example, I was 37 years old and I wanted 35 to 40 percent of my portfolio to be comprised of bonds. But the rapidly rising stock market in 2007 was sending my stock indexes far higher than the allocation I set for them. As a result, my bonds represented far less than 35 percent of my total account, so I spent 2007 buying bonds—even selling some of my stock indexes to do it.

I resumed my aggressive stock-buying plan in 2008 when the stock market traded at a 20 percent discount to its 2007 peak. Figure 4.3 shows what kind of hammering the stock market took in 2008. And I happily increased my purchases with my monthly savings as the markets plummeted by 50 percent from 2007 to a low point in March 2009. It was like wandering into an Apple computer dealership and seeing the discount bins filled to the brim with the latest iPhones. Stocks were selling at 50 percent off—and nobody was lining up to buy them! At one point, the stock indexes had fallen so far that I sold a large amount of my bond index so I could buy more of my stock index, mindful of keeping a balanced allocation of stocks and bonds. When the stock markets fell, my bond allocation ended up being significantly higher than 35 percent of my total portfolio. Selling off some of my bond index to buy more of my stock index also helped bring my portfolio back to the desired allocation.

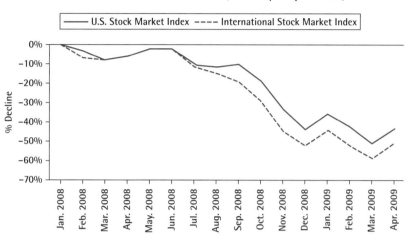

Figure 4.3 Worldwide Stock Market Sale
Source: Vanguard historical prices for total U.S. and international indexes

With stock prices falling so heavily, I finally understood Buffett's comments in 1974 when he was interviewed by *Forbes* magazine. Faced at the time with a stock market drop of a similar magnitude, he said he felt like an oversexed guy in a harem.[13]

Again, did the economic downturn in 2008–2009 eat into the profits of U.S. businesses? Certainly some of them lost money, but not all. If stock prices fall by 50 percent, it can only be justified if business earnings have fallen (or expected to fall) by 50 percent. As always with the stock market, investors' fear and greed can produce irrational price levels. In 2008–2009, I prayed stocks would remain cheap.

Obviously, praying for something so nonspiritual was the wrong thing to do. Perhaps divine intervention punished me for it when the markets rose. Between March 2009 and January 2011, the U.S. stock market index rose 85 percent and the international stock market index, which I was also buying, rose nearly 90 percent. I'm not the sort of guy who normally gets depressed, but the indexes I was buying were getting pricier by the month. I would have preferred it if the markets had stayed low.

People don't normally get such wonderful opportunities to take advantage of crazy, short-term discounts. But with sensational financial television programs based on financial Armageddon, with a rough economic period, and with the Internet spreading news of emotional market sentiment far and wide, we had a recipe for some remarkable stock market volatility over the past decade.

Most people, unfortunately, are easily conquered by their enemy in the mirror. They like buying stock market investments when prices are rising, and they shrink away in horror when they see bargains. How do we know? We just need to observe what most investors do when stock markets are falling or rising. John Bogle, in his classic text, *Common Sense on Mutual Funds,* reveals the startling data while asking the rhetorical question: "Will investors never learn?"

In the late 1990s, when stock markets were defying gravity, investors piled more money into the stock market than they ever had before, adding $650 billion to stock mutual funds during this period. Then when stock prices became cheap in 2008 and 2009 with the biggest market decline since 1929–1933, what do you think most American mutual fund investors were doing? When they should have been enthusiastically buying, they were selling off more than $228 billion of stock market mutual funds.[14]

What we do know about the future is that we will once again experience unpredictable stock market shockers. The markets will either fall, seemingly off a cliff, or they'll catch hold of a rocket to soar into the stratosphere. Armed with the knowledge of how stock markets reflect business earnings you won't be seduced to take silly risks, and you won't be as fearful when markets fall. By building a responsible portfolio of stock and bond indexes, you'll create more stability in your account while providing opportunities to take advantage of stock market silliness.

The next chapter will show you in detail how to achieve this in the simplest, possible way.

Notes

1. John C. Bogle, *The Little Book of Common Sense Investing* (Hoboken, New Jersey: John Wiley & Sons, 2007), 51.
2. Ibid.
3. John C. Bogle, *Common Sense on Mutual Funds* (Hoboken, New Jersey: John Wiley & Sons, 2010), 28.

4. Jeremy Siegel, *Stocks for the Long Run* (New York: McGraw-Hill, 2002), 217–218.

5. Ken Fisher, *The Only Three Questions That Count* (Hoboken, New Jersey: John Wiley & Sons, 2007), 279.

6. Ibid.

7. "Coca-Cola Report," The Value Line Investment Survey, November 9, 2001, 1551.

8. "Long Term Performance of Major Developed Equity Markets," Management and Factset Research Systems, accessed April 15, 2011, http://www.fulcrumasset.com/files/Long%20Term%20Equity%20Performance.PDF.

9. Quote DB, accessed April 15, 2011, http://www.quotedb.com/quotes/3038.

10. "A Long-Term Perspective Chart," The Value Line Investment Survey, 1920–2005.

11. Burton Malkiel, *A Random Walk Down Wall Street* (New York: WW Norton & Company, 2003), 86.

12. Lawrence Cunningham, *The Essays of Warren Buffett* (Singapore: John Wiley & Sons, 2009), 86–87.

13. Forbes, from the archives, "Warren Buffett—1974," accessed on January 5, 2011, http://www.forbes.com/2008/04/30/warren-buffett-profile-invest-oped-cx_hs_0430buffett.html.

14. John C. Bogle, *Common Sense on Mutual Funds*, 32.

RULE 5

Build Mountains of Money with a Responsible Portfolio

"Eat your Brussels sprouts," I used to hear when I was a kid, "and you'll grow into a big, strong boy."

So I ate a bowl of Brussels sprouts for breakfast, a plate of Brussels sprouts for lunch, and a casserole dish of Brussels sprouts for dinner—seven days a week.

If that were true, I'd probably resemble a green, leafy ball with legs by now. Brussels sprouts might be good for you, but you need to eat more than a bunch of tiny cabbages if you want to be healthy.

In the same vein, a total stock market index fund might be good for you as well, but it doesn't represent a balanced portfolio.

If that were all you bought, your portfolio would gyrate wildly with the stock market. If the market dropped 20 percent, so would your overall portfolio. If the market dropped 50 percent, so would your total investments.

This isn't good for any investor, especially those approaching retirement and needing more stability. If a 60-year-old plans to use her portfolio as a nest egg, she's not going to be comfortable seeing all of her hard-earned money plunge into what might look like a bottomless crater during a sharp market decline.

Only an irresponsible portfolio would fall 50 percent if the stock market value were cut in half. That's because bonds become parachutes when stock markets fall.

What Are Bonds?

Bond is a secret British agent with a license to kill. He sleeps with multiple women, never dies, and every 15 years or so, gets a body transplant to look like a completely different guy.

Financial bonds are just as riveting.

Bonds get less shaken and stirred

Long term, bonds don't make as much money as stocks. But they're less volatile, so they can save your account from falling to the bottom of a stock market canyon if the market gods feel like purging for fun.

A bond is a loan that you make to a government or a corporation. Your money is safe as long as that entity (the government or the corporation receiving the loan) is able to pay the money back, plus annual interest.

The safest ones you can buy are first-world government bonds from high-income industrial countries. Slightly riskier bonds can be bought from strong blue-chip businesses such as Coca-Cola <www.coca-cola.com>, Wal-Mart <www.walmart.com>, and Johnson & Johnson <www.jnj.com>.

Riskier bonds pay higher interest, but there's a higher chance that they might forfeit on the loan. The higher the interest paid by a corporate bond, the higher the risk associated with it.

If you're looking for a safe place for your money, it's best to keep it in short-term government bonds or short-term, high-quality corporate bonds.

Why short-term? If you buy a bond paying four percent annually over the next 10 years, there's always a chance that inflation could make a meal out of it. If that happens, you're essentially losing money. Sure, the bond is paying you four percent annually, but if you're buying breakfast cereal that increases in price every year by six percent, then your four percent bond interest is losing to a box of cornflakes.

For this reason, buying bonds with shorter maturities (such as one- to three-year bonds) is wiser than buying longer term bonds (such as 10-year bonds). If inflation rears its head, you won't be saddled with a 10-year commitment to a certain interest rate. When a short-term bond expires, and you get your money back, you can buy another short-term bond at the higher interest rate.

If this sounds complicated, don't worry. You can buy a short-term government bond index, and you never have to worry about an expiration date. It will keep pace with inflation over time, and you can sell it whenever you want. It's easy.

If you want to know how bonds work, here's the skinny

You don't need to know the intricacies of how bonds work. You can just buy a government bond index (which I'll show you how to do in the next chapter) and that bond index can represent the temperate part of your investment account. But if you want to know how bonds work, here it is in a half-page nutshell:

If you bought a five-year government bond, you would know immediately what the interest rate would be, and that the rate would be guaranteed by the government. If you loaned a government say, $10,000, they would promise to give you that $10,000 back. Along the way, you would be guaranteed to earn $500 each year in interest payments, assuming that the interest rate was five percent annually.

If you choose to sell that bond before the five years are up, you can do that, but bond prices fluctuate every day. Instead of getting back your $10,000, you might get back $10,500 or $9,500, if you sell before the maturity date.

When inflation/interest rates rise, bond prices fall. If inflation were running at three percent annually when you bought a bond that yields five percent in interest, and if inflation suddenly jumped to five percent, then no new investors would want to buy a bond like yours (paying five percent interest with inflation at five percent.) If they did, they wouldn't make any money after the increase in the cost of living. But if the price of that bond dropped, the new investor would be lured by the idea of paying $9,500 for the same bond that you paid $10,000. When that bond expired, the new investor would get $10,000 back.

If interest rates dropped, a friend of yours might be dying to buy your $10,000 bond that pays five percent in interest annually. But he wouldn't be alone. Institutional bond traders would rush to buy that bond quickly, resulting in a price increase for it—perhaps from $10,000 to $10,300. Bond-price adjustments are similar to stock-price adjustments. If there's more demand, the price will rise.

Your friend, however, would earn five percent annually on $10,000 (not on the $10,300 he paid for the bond). When the bond expired, he would receive $10,000 back. You'd brag. He'd get upset. And if your friend were anything like my dad, you would find cat food in your shoes the following morning.

You can see why there's a bond "trading market" as people try to take advantage of these price movements. It only follows that there are actively managed mutual funds focused on buying and selling bonds as well.

Bond index funds are the winner

In case you're tempted to buy an actively managed bond fund, remember this: bond index funds beat them silly. Costs matter even more in the world of bond funds.

Figure 5.1 reveals that from 2003 to 2008, the average actively managed government bond fund with a sales load (that crafty commission paid to advisers) made 3.7 percent annually and the

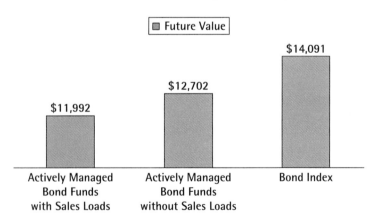

Actively Managed Bond Funds vs. Indexed Bond Funds (2003-2008)

☐ Future Value

$14,091

$12,702

$11,992

Actively Managed	Actively Managed	Bond Index
Bond Funds	Bond Funds	
with Sales Loads	without Sales Loads	

Figure 5.1 Comparison of Funds

Source: John C Bogle, *Common Sense on Mutual Funds*

average actively managed bond fund without a sales load made 4.9 percent annually. As with actively managed stock market mutual funds, those without sales-load fees outperform, on average, those with sales-load fees.

During the same period, a U.S. government bond index averaged 7.1 percent annually. Whether you're buying stock indexes or bond indexes, active management generally slashes your return potential because of the hidden fees associated with them.[1]

Ensuring that your account has a bond index, a domestic stock index, and an international stock index provides you with a greater statistical chance of investment success.

What percentage of your portfolio should you have in bonds?

The debate over what percentage you should own in stocks and what percentage you should own in bonds is livelier than an Italian family reunion.

A rule of thumb is that you should have a bond allocation that's roughly equivalent to your age. Some experts suggest that it should be your age minus 10, or if you want a riskier portfolio, your age minus 20; for example, a 50-year-old would have between 30 and 50 percent of his or her investment portfolio in bonds.

Common sense should be used here. A 50-year-old government employee expecting a guaranteed pension when he retires can afford to invest less than 50 percent of his portfolio in bonds. He can take on greater risk (on the promise of higher returns). Stock returns don't always beat bond returns over the short term, but over long periods, stocks run circles around bonds. That said, bonds could be your secret weapon when stocks hit the skids.

Trounce the professionals with a balanced portfolio

If you're adding $200 a month to a portfolio, you could add $60 a month to a bond index ($60 is 30 percent of $200) and $140 a month ($140 is 70 percent of $200) to your stock indexes.

In any given year, as you know, the stock market can go crazy, rising or dropping by 30 percent or more. Dispassionate, intelligent investors can simply rebalance their portfolios if they're too far from the stock/bond allocation they set for themselves.

For example, if a 30-year-old man has 30 percent in bonds and 70 percent in stocks, he will want to maintain that allocation.

If the stock market falls heavily in a given month, the investor will find that his portfolio (which started out with 70 percent in stocks) now has a lower percentage in stocks than his goal allocation of 70 percent. So what should that investor do when adding fresh money to the account? He should add to his stock indexes.

If the stock market rose considerably during another month, the investor might find that stocks now make up more than 70 percent of his total portfolio. What should he do with fresh money? He should add to his bond index.

Profiting from Panic—Stock Market Crash 2008–2009

When stock markets fall, most people panic, sending stocks to lower levels. Dispassionate investors, however, can lay the groundwork for significant future profits. My personal portfolio was far larger after the financial crisis compared with its level before the crisis scuttled the markets. Following the strategy to keep my personal portfolio aligned with my desired allocation of stocks and bonds was the key. As I mentioned in the previous chapter, I started 2008 (before the stock market crash) with a bond allocation at roughly 35 percent of my total portfolio as shown in Figure 5.2.

My Portfolio—January 2008

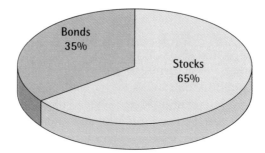

Bonds
35%

Stocks
65%

Figure 5.2 Portfolio at Age 37

My Portfolio–January 2009

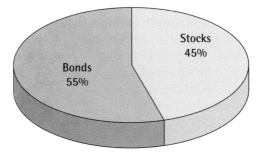

Figure 5.3   Portfolio at Age 38

Then the stock markets started falling, giving me a disproportionate percentage in bonds. I invest monthly, so when the markets fell—to keep me close to my desired stock/bond allocation—I bought nothing but stocks and stock indexes. But no matter how much money I was adding to my stock indexes, the markets continued to drop heavily during the end of 2008 and the beginning of 2009.

Figure 5.3 shows what my portfolio was looking like during the first few months of 2009.

Despite my monthly stock market purchases, I couldn't get my stock allocation back to 65 percent of my total. As a result, I had to sell some of my bonds in early 2009 to bring my portfolio back to my desired allocation.

Naturally, I was hoping the markets would stay low. But they didn't. As the stock markets began recovering later that year, I switched tactics again and bought nothing but bonds for more than a year. I was low on bonds because I had sold bonds to buy stocks, and my stocks were rising in value.

This kind of rebalancing is common practice among university endowment funds and pension funds.

Usually investors don't need to address their stock/bond allocation more than once a year. But when the stock markets go completely nuts—dropping by 20 percent or more—it's a good idea to take advantage of it if you can.

Having a Foreign Affair

Americans should have a nice chunk of money in a U.S. index; Canadians should have a good-sized chunk in a Canadian index; and so it should follow for Australians, Brits, Singaporeans, or any other nationality with an established stock market. An investor's portfolio should always have the home country index represented. After all, it makes sense to keep much of your money in the currency with which you pay your bills.

After adding a government bond index to your portfolio, you really could stop right there.

But many investors (me included) like having an international component to their portfolios. The U.S. stock market makes up just 45 percent of the world's stock market exposure. There are stock markets in Canada, Australia, England, France, Japan, and China, just to mention a few, and it's advantageous to get exposure to the other 55 percent of the world's stock markets.

A total international stock market index would fit the bill.

There are many trains of thought relating to how much of your stock exposure should be international. To keep it simple, you could split your stock market money between your home country index and an international index.

In that case, a 30-year-old American investor (without an upcoming pension) would have a portfolio that looked like the one on Figure 5.4:

Investment Portfolio of a 30-Year-Old

Figure 5.4 Investment Portfolio Percentages

If you're making monthly investment purchases, you need to look at your home country stock index and your international stock index and determine which one has done better over the previous month. When you figure it out (hold on for this!) you need to add newly invested money to the index that hasn't done as well to keep your account close to your desired allocation.

What do most people do? You guessed it. Metaphorically speaking, they sign long-term future contracts to empty their wallets each morning into the toilet—buying more of the high-performing index and less of the underperforming index. Over an investment lifetime, behavior such as this can cost hundreds of thousands of dollars.

Over my lifetime, the total U.S. stock market index and the total international stock market index have performed similarly. There's less than one percent compounding difference between the two since 1970.[1] But there are times when one will lag the other. Take advantage of that.

Please note that I'm not talking about chasing individual stocks or individual foreign markets into the gutter. For example, just because the share price of company "Random X" has fallen doesn't mean that investors should throw good money after bad, thinking that it's a great deal just because it has dropped in value. Who knows what's going to happen to "Random X." It could vaporize like a San Francisco fog.

Likewise, you take a large risk buying an index focusing on a single foreign country, such as Chile, Brazil, or China. Who really knows what's going to happen to those markets over the next 30 years? They might do really well, but it's better to spread your risk and go with the total international stock market index (if you want foreign exposure). Within it, you'll have exposure to older world economies such as England, France, and Germany, as well as the younger, fast-growing economies of China, India, Brazil, and Thailand. Just remember to rebalance. If the international stock market goes on a tear, don't chase it with fresh money. If your domestic stock index and the international stock index both shoot skyward, add fresh money to your bond index.

If that sounds too complicated, Scott Burns has popularized an even simpler strategy.

Introducing the Couch Potato Portfolio

A former columnist with *The Dallas Morning News*, Burns now works with AssetBuilder, a U.S.-based investment company that manages money with indexed strategies. Recognizing that actively managed mutual fund purchases didn't make sense (thanks to high fees, high-tax consequences, and poor performance), he popularized a simple investment strategy called The Couch Potato Portfolio.

It's comprised of an equal commitment to a U.S. total stock market index and a total bond market index. In other words, if you were investing $200 a month, you would put $100 a month into the stock market index and $100 a month into the bond market index. You don't even have to open your investment statements more than once a year if you don't want.

After one year is up, look at your investment account and figure out whether you now have more money in stocks or bonds. If there's more money in the bond index, sell some of it to get equal weighting in your portfolio, buying the stock index with the proceeds. If there's more money in the stock index, sell some of your stock market index and buy the bond index with the proceeds.

Without allowing yourself to fall victim to the crazy "ups and downs" of the markets, you would be buying low and selling high once a year.

With a 50 percent bond component, this would be a pretty conservative account. If the stock markets fell by 50 percent in a given year, your account would fall far less than that and you would have a chance to even out your account 12 months later by buying the underpriced stock index with proceeds from the bond index.

Such a strategy, despite its very conservative nature, would have averaged 10.96 percent annually from 1986 to 2001.[2]

This would have turned $1,000 into $4,758.79 over that 15-year period.

But a drunken monkey tossing darts at the stock market page could have made decent money from 1986 to 2001 because most of the world's stock markets rose significantly during that time. How did the indexed couch potato strategy perform when stock markets went through their gut-wrenching dives and rises (and dives again) during the past 10 years—a decade that many stock market investors have coined "the lost decade"? For starters, the indexed couch potato strategy let investors sleep more soundly during market drops, thanks to the large bond component.

During 2002, the U.S. stock market was hammered and the average U.S. stock market mutual fund declined 22.8 percent in value. In other words, an investment of $10,000 would have fallen to $7,723. But during that devastating year, the markets were only able to knock the couch potato strategy down 6.9 percent. A $10,000 investment would have dropped to $9,310.[3]

Between the beginning of 2003 and the beginning of 2008, the U.S. and international stock market indexes rose dramatically, gaining 91 percent and 186 percent respectively.[4] If you had money in the markets during these five years, you probably would have increased your portfolio size exponentially, no matter who was managing it. But let's have a look at one of the ugliest years in modern financial history: 2008.

With the global economic crisis, world stock markets took a beating. Of course, long-term investors would have been gleefully rubbing their hands as they took advantage of the lower stock prices, but let's see how the average U.S. mutual fund and the couch potato concept would have fared during that falling market.

If you thought the average professional could have weathered the storm, you'd be disappointed. Table 5.1 shows that the average actively managed stock market mutual fund (comprised of stocks, without bonds) dropped 29.1 percent in 2008, compared to a drop of 20.4 percent for the indexed couch potato portfolio. And how about the average actively managed balanced fund? Balanced funds don't have the same kind of exposure to the stock market that regular stock market mutual funds have. Balanced funds are usually comprised of 60 percent stocks and 40 percent bonds. When stocks fell dramatically in 2008, the bond component of the average actively managed balanced fund should have cushioned the fall. But that wasn't the case. The average actively managed balanced fund dropped a whopping 28 percent during 2008.[6] Why did the average balanced fund manager lose so much money even though 40 percent to 50 percent of their funds' assets were in bonds? The only explanation is that they were afraid, and they sold

Table 5.1   The Couch Potato Portfolio vs. the Average U.S. Mutual Fund in 2008[5]

The Average U.S. Mutual Fund	-29.1% drop	$10,000 dropped to $7,090
The Indexed Couch Potato Portfolio Concept	-20.4% drop	$10,000 dropped to $7,960

stocks when the markets fell. As mentioned in my previous chapter, nobody can predict the short-term movements of the stock markets. It's likely that most of the actively managed balanced fund managers in the U.S. were trying to do exactly that—with expensive consequences for their investors, as they sold stocks when prices were low. Following a disciplined couch potato strategy is likely to be far more profitable than allowing a fund manager to mess with your money.

Another nice thing about using the couch potato portfolio strategy is that (despite the market crash of 2008–2009) you would have still made money from 2006–2011. During this five-year period—when many actively managed balanced mutual funds lost money—a $10,000 investment in the couch potato portfolio would have grown to more than $12,521.56 without adding money to it. That's an overall gain of 25.2 percent.[7]

As an investor, I loved the stock market decline of 2008–2009. But as a consultant, it was disheartening. Many people brought their portfolios to me during the economic crisis, revealing investments that had collapsed 40 percent or more in value.

When I looked at their investment holdings, I found something pretty shocking: their investment advisers obviously had little respect for bonds. Most of the people who showed me their statements were older than me, so they should have had bond components that equaled or exceeded mine. But none did. In some cases, they had no bonds at all! Their accounts fell far further than mine when the markets declined and they couldn't take advantage of cheap stock market prices because they didn't have any bonds to sell.

Investors in their 50s and 60s, especially, require bonds in their portfolios. It would be tough to find an investment book that didn't include this fundamental principle. But many of the accounts I saw were fully exposed to the market's gyrations without a protective bond component.

I teach with one fellow whom I refer to as a "cowboy investor." He's in his mid-50s, and won't have a pension because he spent his career teaching in private schools overseas. He says bonds are for wimps, so he doesn't own any. Buying whatever rises in value (after it rises) and selling whatever falls (after it falls) gives him the distinction of a cowboy who'll never have enough money to leave the ranch.

Combinations of Stocks and Bonds Can Have Powerful Returns

Even when stock markets are rising, a portfolio with a bond component isn't the "party pooper" most cowboy investors think it is. Financial author Daniel Solin notes that from 1973 to 2004, an investor with an allocation of 60 percent in a U.S. stock market index and 40 percent in a total bond market index would have earned an average return of 10.49 percent annually.

An investor taking much more risk and having 100 percent of their portfolio in a stock index would have returns averaging 11.19 percent annually during this period.[8]

The cowboy investor would have taken on more risk, and for what? An extra 0.7 percent annual return? He would need to have a strong stomach. Table 5.2 demonstrates that his worst year during this 31-year time period would have seen his account plunge by 20.15 percent. In contrast, an account with 40 percent bonds and 60 percent stocks wouldn't have fallen further than 9.15 percent during its worst 12 months.[9]

If that extra 0.7 percent return annually is worth the stomach-churning volatility, then go for it. But keep in mind that doing so won't allow you to rebalance your account by taking advantage of cheap stock prices when they offer a sale.

When bonds whip cowboys

The premise of rebalancing stock and bond indexes doesn't just work in the United States. The fundamental principle works no matter where you're investing. *MoneySense* magazine's founding editor, Ian McGugan, won a Canadian National Magazine Award for an article adapting the couch potato strategy for Canadians. His

Table 5.2   Mixed Bag of Stocks and Bonds

1973–2004 100% stocks	60% Stocks/40% bonds
11.19% annual return	10.49% annual return
Worst year: −20.15%	Worst year: −9.15%

method was simple. An investor splits money evenly between a U.S. stock market index, a Canadian stock market index, and a bond market index.

At the end of the calendar year, the investor simply rebalances the portfolio back to the original allocation. If the U.S. stock market index did better than the Canadian index, then the investor would sell some of the U.S. index to even things out with the Canadian index.

If the bond index beat both stock indexes, then some of the bond index would be sold to buy some of the Canadian and U.S. stock market indexes. Of course, if you're making monthly contributions to the account, you could rebalance monthly by simply buying the laggard—to keep your allocation evenly split three ways.

(*MoneySense* tracks a portfolio following this strategy online at the following link: <www.moneysense.ca/2006/04/05/classic-couch-potato-portfolio-historical-performance-tables/>).

You can see, in Table 5.3, how $100 invested in 1975 would have grown if it was rebalanced annually with equal allocations to the Canadian stock index, the U.S. stock index, and the Canadian bond index. Note that from 1975 to the end of 2010, a combination of bond indexes and stock market indexes wasn't just "for wimps." The rebalancing combination of indexes with bonds actually beat the returns of the Canadian stock market index. You really can employ the safety of bonds and enjoy some decent returns in the process.

Table 5.3   Invested in the Canadian Couch Potato Portfolio vs. Canadian Stock Index (1975–2010)

Year	Canadian Couch Potato Portfolio	Canadian Stock Index
1975	$100	$100
1976	$118	$100
1981	$195	$257
1986	$475	$469
1991	$730	$615
1996	$1,430	$1,134
2001	$2,268	$1,525
2006	$3,163	$2,725
2010	$3,493	$3,157

Source: Moneysense.ca (1976–2009 data) Globeinvestor.com (2009–2010 data)[10]

Creating a disciplined plan to rebalance a portfolio removes the guesswork from investing, and it forces investors to ignore their hearts. As I mentioned before, we don't tend to be rational. Most people like buying shares that have risen in value and they like selling shares that have fallen in value. Smart investors don't behave so irrationally.

Contrary to what many people think, beating a 100 percent stock market index is possible over time using bond indexes as your little helpers. You will end up with less volatility and the possibility of better returns.

Notes

1. David Swensen, *Pioneering Portfolio Management* (New York: Free Press, 2009), 170.
2. Paul Farrell, *The Lazy Person's Guide to Investing* (New York: Warner Business Books, 2004), 12.
3. Scott Burns, "Couch Potato Didn't Do the Market Mash," February 2, 2003, *Dallas News* online, accessed November 1, 2010, http://www.dallasnews.com/s/dws/bus/scottburns/couch potato/columns/stories/020203dnbizburnscol.d6d1e.html.
4. Morningstar data for VTSMX (Vanguard total stock market index) and VGTSX (Vanguard total international stock market index) 2003–2008.
5. Scott Burns, "Sloth Triumphs Again," UExpress.com, February 15, 2009, accessed November 1, 2010, http://www.uexpress.com/ scottburns/index.html?uc_full_date=20090215.
6. Ibid.
7. "Monthly Self Managed Couch Potato Returns," AssetBuilder, accessed January 16, 2011, http://assetbuilder.com/couch_potato/ couch_potato_results.aspx.
8. Daniel Solin, *The Smartest Investment Book You'll Ever Read* (New York: Penguin, 2006), 63–64.
9. Ibid., 63.
10. "Couch Potato Performance," *MoneySense* online, accessed November 1, 2010, http://www.moneysense.ca/2006/04/05/ classic-couch-potato-portfolio-historical-performance-tables/.

Sample a "Round-the-World" Ticket to Indexing

Contrary to what some investment books have inadvertently led you to conclude, index funds have boarded ships and airplanes to find happy homes outside of the United States. In this section, I'll give you examples of how to build an indexed account whether you live in the U.S., Canada, Singapore, or Australia. Feel free to check out the section relating to your geographic area, or read with interest how our international brothers and sisters can create indexed accounts. Even if you live in a country not mentioned here, as long as you have the ability to open a brokerage account in your home country, you can build a portfolio of indexes.

The people I'm profiling below are real. These are their real names—and their real stories.

Indexing in the United States—An American Father of Triplets

When Kris Olson's wife, Erica, had triplets in 2006, she single-handedly gave birth to a quarter of a soccer team. Suddenly, there were three more mouths to feed, a minivan to buy, and three college educations to save for.

I'm not suggesting that anyone would hold a charitable benefit with accompanying violin music for a well-paid specialist in pediatrics and internal medicine. But if you're American, and suddenly more aware of your own financial obligations, Kris' story of opening an indexed investing account could provide some direction.

The 40-year-old doctor realized that investing money was similar, in many ways, to the global health work he does in the poverty-stricken, tsunami-affected regions of Sumatra, Indonesia, where he occasionally flies to train midwives. This latest passion comes on the tail of his volunteer work along the Thai-Burmese border, as well as in Darfur, Cambodia, Kenya, and Ethiopia.

Realizing that donations to developing countries are best done in person, he and his wife Erica (a registered nurse) often brought their own medical supplies to the countries they visited. Simply sending supplies was an invitation for third-world middlemen to plunder the goods before they arrived.

In 2004, Kris recognized that something similar was happening to his investments at home, which had been laboring in actively managed mutual funds for years.

"My financial adviser was a really nice guy, but I realize that he skimmed money off me like guys at a third-world country border. I was flushing money down the toilet in tiny sums that were adding up," he said.

On a trip to Indonesia, Kris made a stopover in Singapore, where he purchased cardiopulmonary resuscitation (CPR) training material to take to midwives in Aceh. I met him for lunch at a Japanese restaurant, and over sushi, he asked me what indexes he should buy for his investment account.

The largest index provider in the U.S. is Vanguard, a nonprofit investment company based in Pennsylvania. If you go to their website, the array of indexes can be confusing at first. But I suggested that Kris—who was 35 years old at the time—should keep things simple: buy the broadest stock index he could for his U.S. exposure, the broadest international index he could for his "world" exposure, and a total bond market index fund that approximated his age. Here's the allocation I recommended:

- 35% Vanguard U.S. Bond Index (Symbol VBMFX)
- 35% Vanguard Total U.S. Stock Market Index (Symbol VTSMX)
- 30% Vanguard Total International Stock Market Index (Symbol VGTSX)

I gave my advice on this basis: Vanguard doesn't charge commissions to buy or sell; he would be diversified across the entire U.S.

stock market and the international stock markets; and he would have a bond allocation that would allow him to rebalance his account annually.

"Kris," I said, "don't listen to Wall Street, don't read financial newspapers, and don't watch stock market-based news. If you rebalance a portfolio like this just once a year, you'll beat 90 percent of investment professionals over time."

When Kris got back home to the U.S., he put his old mutual fund investment statements on the dining room table, logged on to the Vanguard site, and telephoned the company from the website's contact information.

A Vanguard employee walked Kris through the account opening process as they negotiated the website together. She simply asked for his existing mutual fund account numbers—for both his IRA account (a tax-sheltered individual retirement account) and for his non-IRA mutual funds.

Over the telephone, the Vanguard representative then transferred his assets from his previous fund company to Vanguard where he diversified his money into the three index funds. Then, after taking his regular bank account information, she set up automatic deposits into Kris's index funds according to the allocation he wanted.

At the end of each calendar year, Kris took a look at his investments. "It didn't take much," he said. "I just rebalanced the portfolio back to the original allocation at the end of each year, (as seen in Figure 6.1) selling off a bit of the 'winners' to bolster the 'losers.' It was the only time I ever looked at my investment statements—just when it was time to consider rebalancing." I was able to confirm Kris's investment returns (in U.S. dollars) using the fund-tracking function at Morningstar.com.

January 2007

Kris noticed that the portfolio he established one year earlier had gained 15.4 percent during the course of the year, with most of the gains coming from his international and U.S. stock market indexes. He called Vanguard on the phone, logged on to his account online, and the Vanguard representative guided him through the process of selling off some of his stock indexes to buy his bond index, bringing him back to his desired allocation. Kris was ready to tune

Kris's Portfolio

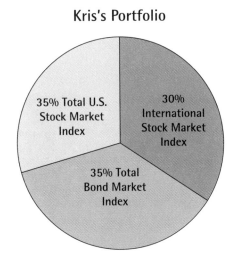

Figure 6.1   Kris Olson's Account Allocation

Wall Street out for another year with his portfolio aligned the way it was when he started.

January 2008

Worldwide, stock markets continued to rise from 2007 to 2008. At this point, Kris's profits had really increased, gaining 25.86 percent from the initial 2006 value and nine percent for the 2007 calendar year. Fighting the urge to buy more of what was propelling his portfolio (his stock indexes), Kris sold off portions of his international and U.S. stock indexes to buy more of his bond index with the proceeds. It didn't require any judgment on his part—he just adjusted his account back to its original allocation.

January 2009

When Kris looked at his statements at the beginning of 2009, he noticed his total portfolio had dropped in value as the biggest stock market decline since 1929–1933 was starting to take its toll. It fell 24.5 percent but Kris just rebalanced his portfolio again, selling off some of his bond index to buy falling U.S. and international stock indexes, bringing it back to the original allocation.

January 2010

Kris knew the stock markets took a real beating during the previous year—everyone was talking about it. But because he sold
off some bonds the previous year to buy stocks, he benefited
from the low stock market levels. By January 2010, his account
had increased 23 percent for the year thanks to the rebounding
stock markets. Once again, Kris took 10 minutes in January to
rebalance his account, selling some stock indexes to buy more
of his bond index. When Kris was finished, he was back to his
original allocation.

January 2011

By January 2011, Kris' account had gained another 11.6 percent
over the previous 12 months. From January 1, 2006, until January 1,
2011, his account's profits had increased by 30.7 percent, despite
going through the worst stock market decline (2008–2009) in
many years.[1] Rebalancing once again, he sold off some of his stock
indexes to buy some more of his bond index. Considering that Kris
is now 40 years old, he should be increasing his bond allocation
slowly to match his age.

A medical doctor knocks out
the investment professionals

It's fine for Kris's portfolio to have gained 30.7 percent from
January 2006 to January 2011, but how would it have done if it was
professionally managed by a fund manager with his or her pulse on
the markets?

You'd assume that a doctor spending just 10 minutes a year on
his finances would get scalped if he ever challenged the investment
professionals. But here's the rub. If a mutual fund could be managed for free—with no salaries paid to any affiliated employees—
then Kris's odds of beating the professionals with a fully indexed
account would be slightly less than 50-50. (After all, he's paying
rock-bottom fees to own the world's stock and bond markets, and
only about 50 percent of actively managed stock market money

will beat the market [before fees].) However, by factoring in the real fees of active management along with taxes, the good doctor operates in a climate where the odds are significantly in his favor— if he indexes his money.

Because Kris's account is balanced between stocks and bonds, we can check his performance, in Figure 6.2 compared with three of the best known balanced mutual funds in the U.S.: Fidelity Balanced Fund <http://fundresearch.fidelity.com/ mutual-funds/summary/316345206>, T. Rowe Price Balanced Fund <http://corporate.troweprice.com/ccw/home.do>, and American Funds Balanced Fund <www.americanfunds.com>.

Each of these funds had teams of researchers coming to work each day to juggle their fund holdings, trying to make the best possible returns. But that all costs money, as you know. As a result, Kris beat each of them handily over the past five years by 11.3 percent, 6.68 percent, and 17.57 percent, respectively.

Will he beat all of them every year? Certainly not. But over time, he's likely to pull further and further ahead. Are there balanced funds in the U.S. that beat Kris's returns over the past five years? Sure there are. But we have no way of knowing which funds will beat Kris over the next five years, so Kris's smartest choice is to keep his balanced portfolio of indexes.

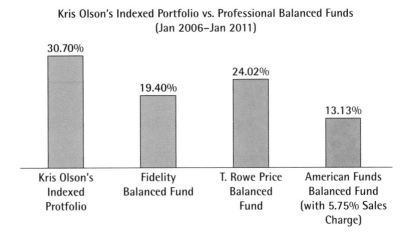

Kris Olson's Indexed Portfolio vs. Professional Balanced Funds
(Jan 2006–Jan 2011)

Figure 6.2   Indexed Portfolio Beats Balanced Funds (2006–2011)
Source: Morningstar.com[2]

Where Vanguard makes things even easier

If the idea of spending 10 minutes a year rebalancing your portfolio is too much, Americans can opt for something even easier. Vanguard offers products called Target Retirement Funds, which offer a blended combination of stock and bond indexes. They're supposed to shift slightly more money into bonds as you get closer to retirement without the investor having to raise a finger to rebalance.

The funds are named based on your projected retirement date, but ignore the named date on the fund. For example, Kris would likely choose the Target Retirement 2015 Fund <https://personal.vanguard.com> because 40 percent of it is allocated toward bonds and Kris is now 40 years old. He isn't really planning to retire in 2015, but he would choose this fund because it has a bond allocation that matches his age.

Between January 2006 and January 2011, Vanguard's Target Retirement 2015 Fund gained 24.14 percent, a return that also beat each of the big three balanced funds found in Figure 6.2: Fidelity Balanced Fund, T. Rowe Price Balanced Fund, and American Funds Balanced Fund.

What's more, if held in a taxable account, the Target Retirement Funds are much more efficient than most (if not all) actively balanced funds. In Table 6.1, you can see the respective "turnover" rates for each of the balanced funds we compared with Kris's account. And remember, the lower the turnover, the higher the tax efficiency.

An array of Vanguard's Target Retirement Funds, with their respective bond allocations and portfolio turnover rates is shown in Table 6.2. Remember not to get too concerned by the target date in the name. If you're a 50-year-old without a pension, it's wise to select a portfolio (or a fund, in this case) that has a bond allocation somewhat

Table 6.1 Turnover Rate of Respective Funds

Balanced / Target Retirement Funds	Taxable Turnover (the Lower, the Better)
Vanguard Target Retirement 2015 Fund	19%
Fidelity Balanced Fund	122%
American Funds Balanced Fund	46%
T. Rowe Price Balanced Fund	41%

Source: Morningstar.com[3]

Table 6.2   Turnover Rate of Vanguard's Target Retirement Funds

Vanguard Target Retirement Funds	Bonds/Cash	Turnover
Target Retirement 2005 Fund	64.5%	21%
Target Retirement 2010 Fund	50.6%	19%
Target Retirement 2015 Fund	40.3%	19%
Target Retirement 2020 Fund	33%	14%
Target Retirement 2025 Fund	25.4%	11%
Target Retirement 2030 Fund	18.2%	13%
Target Retirement 2035 Fund	10.7%	9%
Target Retirement 2040 Fund	10.3%	9%

Source: Morningstar.com[4]

equivalent to your age. If, however, you're expecting to enjoy a generous pension upon retirement, you can afford to take greater risks by choosing a target fund with a lower bond component.

The United States is one of the easiest countries from which to build an investment account of indexes. And the options are rapidly growing for non-Americans as well.

Indexing In Canada—A Landscaper Wins by Pruning Costs

Originally from Rotorua, New Zealand, a beautiful city built at the bottom of an old volcanic crater, Keith Wakelin's family moved to British Columbia, Canada, when he was a teenager.

As a keen, long-distance runner, he made a name for himself as a tough competitor who has been racing toward finish lines for nearly four decades. When he was 42, he won Vancouver's body-destroying 50-kilometer Knee Knackering Mountain Race in 2000. At 52, he's still a competitive force to be reckoned with.

Keith soon recognized that investing and distance running shared common ground. You can't carry excess weight if you want to be fast over long distances. And if you want to increase your odds of growing rich, you can't carry the burden of excess financial costs.

Wanting to diversify across all markets, Keith bought a total international stock market index, a Canadian stock market index, a U.S. stock market index, and a Canadian bond market index.

Table 6.3   The Global Couch Potato Portfolio

Index	Percentage in Each	Identifying Ticker Symbol
International Stock Market Index	20%	XIN
Canadian Stock Market Index	20%	XIC
U.S. Stock Market Index	20%	XSP
Canadian Bond Market Index	40%	XBB

He simply followed *MoneySense* magazine's global couch potato performance concept, suggesting that you can split your money in the allocations as shown in Table 6.3. *MoneySense* tracks this portfolio online.[5]

At the end of each year, Keith looked at his account's allocation. Each of his indexes performed slightly differently. Taking a few minutes once a year, Keith rebalanced his account back to its original allocation.

By selling off bits of the winners to add to the losers each year, Keith earned a total return of 28.5 percent (in Canadian dollars) from January 2005 to January 2011. This includes the drumming that the world's stock markets took in 2008-2009.[5]

How did Keith's portfolio stack up?

In Canada, there are five main banks, and they have the lion's share of the actively managed mutual fund business:

1. Toronto Dominion Bank (TD Bank) <www.tdcanadatrust.com>

2. Bank of Montreal (BMO) <www.bmo.com/home>

3. Canadian Imperial Bank of Commerce (CIBC) <www.cibc.com>

4. ScotiaBank <www.scotiabank.com>

5. Royal Bank of Canada (RBC) <www.rbc.com>

The closest actively managed funds we have to Keith's portfolio (in terms of how the assets are placed) are with the "Balanced Funds" and each of the Canadian banks above has its Balanced flagship constituting both stocks and bonds.

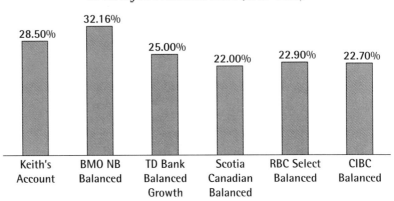

Keith's Index Portfolio vs. Balanced Funds
at the Big Five Canadian Banks (2005–2011)

Figure 6.3   Keith's Account vs. Balanced Funds at the Canadian Banks
(2005–2011)
Source: Globeinvestor.com Fund Performances[6]

How did Keith's account perform compared with the banks?

Of the funds in Figure 6.3, the only one that beat Keith was the Bank of Montreal's NB Balanced Fund. Over a six-year period, Keith beat four out of five of Canada's most respected balanced mutual funds without even trying. Of course, there will be actively managed balanced funds that beat Keith over time, but there's no way of knowing which ones. Next year, for example, the Bank of Montreal Fund, which is in first place now, could find itself trailing all of the other funds. That's how it often works in the fund industry. There's only one thing for sure: Thanks to its low-fee structure, Keith's portfolio will outperform at least 90 percent of actively managed balanced funds. And if his money were held in a taxable account, he would extend his lead over the majority of Canada's actively managed funds.

How can Canadians invest like Keith?

If you want to invest like Keith, you have two low-cost options:

1. You can buy the low-cost Toronto Dominion Bank Index Funds <www.tdcanadatrust.com/mutualfunds/tdeseriesfunds/index.jsp> (called e-Series Funds), which are—as of 2010—Canada's cheapest regular index funds. Or,

2. You can open a discount brokerage account and buy Exchange Traded Index Funds.

Let's focus on the bank indexes first:
Toronto Dominion Bank currently has the most competitively priced index funds in Canada. But if you try walking into a bank and buying them, one of two things might happen to you:

1. The bank representative might try convincing you to buy actively managed funds instead. Or,

2. The representative might try selling you high-cost index funds. <www.tdcanadatrust.com/mutualfunds/tdeseriesfunds/> (Yes, TD Bank sells high-cost indexes as well, charging nearly twice as much as the indexes I recommend below.)

The low-cost indexes are called e-Series Funds and you can only purchase them online at <www.tdcanadatrust.com/mutualfunds/tdeseriesfunds/index.jsp>.[7]

The TD bank e-Series index funds

Table 6.4 reveals that TD Bank's e-Series index funds cost an average expense ratio of just 0.4 percent annually, compared with more than 2.5 percent annually for the average Canadian actively managed fund.[8] Canadian fund costs are reported to be higher than those in any other country, so it's best to avoid getting fleeced.[9] If

Table 6.4   TD Bank's e-Series Fund Fees

TD Bank's e-Series Indexes	Identification Symbols	Annual Expense Ratios
International Stock Index <www.tdcanada trust.com/mutualfunds/perf_EF.jsp>	TDB905	0.50%
Canadian Stock Index <www.tdcanadatrust .com/mutualfunds/perf_EF.jsp>	TDB900	0.31%
U.S. Stock Index <www.tdcanadatrust .com/mutualfunds/perf_EF.jsp>	TDB902	0.33%
Canadian Bond Market Index <www.tdcanada trust.com/mutualfunds/perf_EF.jsp>	TDB909	0.48%

Table 6.5 Recommended Age-Related Portfolio Allocations for Canadians

Age	Canadian Bond Market Index	Canadian Stock Market Index	U.S. Stock Market Index	Total International Stock Market Index
20	10–25%	25–30%	25–30%	25–30%
30	20–35%	20–25%	20–25%	20–25%
40	30–45%	15–20%	15–20%	15–20%
50	40–55%	10–15%	10–15%	10–15%
60	50–65%	10–15%	10–15%	10–15%

you want to invest using the global couch potato strategy with the cheap, e-Series funds, here they are with their respective identification symbols and hidden annual expense ratios.

You'll need a $100 minimum to open the account. If you want to automatically deposit a set amount into each index from your bank account, follow the online procedure. The minimum purchase for automatic deposits is $25 a month, and there are no fees associated with the account—except a two percent withdraw penalty if you sell within 90 days of opening the account.[10]

For the investor looking for low costs and convenience, these funds are the answer, and you can reinvest your dividends for free.

Remember that a good rule of thumb is to be consistent with your allocations. Choose a percentage for each index and balance it annually.

To blend the couch potato formula with the idea that a bond allocation should represent a person's age, I recommend that you choose one of these age-related breakdowns in Table 6.5.

Canadian indexed investing with exchange traded funds

When Keith first opened his indexed investment account, Toronto Dominion Bank didn't offer e-Series Index Funds. Instead, Keith built a portfolio of exchange traded funds (ETFs), which are index funds that are purchased off the stock market exchange using a brokerage firm.

Investing with ETFs might be worthwhile if you're not going to invest regularly in your account or if your account balance is fairly large.

The costs associated with four exchange traded index funds (such as Keith owns) would amount to annual fees of 0.3 percent each year. This is slightly cheaper than TD bank's e-Series Funds, but the savings might not be worth the trouble. You can decide by weighing the relative size of your account with the savings.

On a $100,000 account, ETFs such as Keith's cost $300 a year in hidden expenses.

On a $100,000 account, e-Series indexes would cost $400 a year in hidden expenses.

The $100 annual savings on a $100,000 account wouldn't be worth the hassle if you were adding regularly to your account. Here's why:

If you invest every month, you'll have to pay a brokerage fee of $9.99 for each online purchase with ETFs (and more than that if your account value is below $100,000).

That monthly $9.99 adds up to nearly $120 a year. So if your account value doesn't easily exceed $100,000, you're better off with the e-Series Index Funds because they don't charge a commission to buy or sell.

Table 6.6 shows the costs associated with buying monthly e-Series indexes (which have higher expense ratios but no commission fees) versus buying exchange traded funds (which have lower expense ratios but charge purchase commissions)

Investing in ETFs does have a cost advantage once an investment account clears about $120,000, but it does require a bit more work on the part of the investor. Also, if the investor's account isn't well above $120,000 and if they make more than 12 purchases in a

Table 6.6   Total Costs of an ETF Portfolio vs. a TD Bank e-Series Portfolio

Account Size	Annual Exchange Traded Fund Expense of 0.3%	Annual e-Series Index Expense of 0.4%	Cost to Buy 12X a year for Exchange Traded Funds	Annual Costs/ Savings with Exchange Traded Funds Compared with e-Series Indexes
$100,000	$300	$400	$119.88	($19.88)
$200,000	$600	$800	$119.88	$80.12
$300,000	$900	$1,200	$119.88	$180.12
$400,000	$1,200	$1,600	$119.88	$280.12
$500,000	$1,500	$2,000	$119.88	$380.12
$600,000	$1,800	$2,400	$119.88	$480.12
$700,000	$2,100	$2,800	$119.88	$580.12

year, the cost savings can swing back in favor of the e-Series Funds. Note, from Table 6.6, that a $700,000 ETF account would save $580.12 a year compared with an e-Series indexed account, even after paying $9.99 a month ($119.88 a year) in annual commission fees.

To purchase Exchange Traded Index Funds, an investor has to open a discount brokerage account. There are a variety of Canadian brokerage firms offering this service, including TD Waterhouse, <www.tdcanadatrust.com/easyweb5/start/tdw/get_started .jsp> CIBC's Investor's Edge, <www.investorsedge.cibc.com/ ie/home.jsp> The Royal Bank Action Direct, <www.rbcdirect investing.com/> and Q-trade Investor <www.qtrade.ca/>.

Commission fees differ, but it's a competitive market and fees are falling. If you're still interested in ETFs and you want to buy like Keith, you'll have to purchase the following indexes off the Toronto Stock Exchange, via your brokerage. The initials before each respective index represent the code you'll need to enter (called a ticker symbol) before making each purchase.

- XIU = Canadian Stock Index

- XBB = Canadian Bond Index

- XIN = International Stock Index

- XSP = U.S. Stock Index

Whether you buy the e-Series index funds from TD Bank or whether you opt for brokerage-purchased ETF indexes, you'll beat the pants off the majority of the pros—just as Keith has.

Indexing in Singapore—A Couple Builds a Tiger's Portfolio in the Lion City

Singaporeans looking to invest in low-cost indexes might Google their options online. But like hidden vipers in the jungles of the Lion City, there are snakes in the financial service industry waiting to venomously erode your investment potential. Googling "Singapore Index Funds" will bring you to a company offering index funds that charge nearly one percent a year. That might seem insignificant, and that's exactly what marketers want you to believe. Paying one percent for an index fund can cost you hundreds of thousands of wasted dollars over an investment lifetime.

Singaporean index-fund retailer Fundsupermart <www.fundsu permart.com/main/home/index.svdo> flogs the Infinity Investment Series. It offers a S&P 500 Index Fund <www.fundsupermart.com/ main/fundinfo/viewFund.svdo?sedolnumber=370283#charge> charging 0.97 percent annually (as an expense ratio) and they charge up to an additional two percent front-end sales fee to make the purchase.[11]

Let's assume that two Singaporean sisters decide to invest in a U.S. index. One of them buys the S&P 500 Index Fund through Fundsupermart while the other chooses to go with Vanguard's low-cost S&P 500 Exchange Traded Index Fund that charges just 0.09 percent annually, which they can buy through Singapore's DBS Vickers brokerage firm.[12]

Before fees, each fund would make the same return because they track exactly the same market. Costs, when presented in tiny amounts—like 0.97 percent—look minimal. But they're not. Table 6.7 shows how seemingly small fees can kill investment profits over a lifetime. If the U.S. S&P 500 index makes five percent a

Table 6.7 Two Sisters Invest SGD$20,000

	Sister 1	Sister 2
$20,000 given to each sister to invest for 35 years	Sister 1 invests in an S&P 500 index fund that costs 0.97% annually	Sister 2 invests in a Vanguard S&P 500 exchange traded fund via DBS Vickers that costs 0.09% annually
Assume an 8% return for the S&P 500 index for the next 30 years	Sister 1 makes 7.03% annually after expenses	Sister 2 makes 7.91% annually after expenses
How much will each sister have after 35 years?	Sister 1 will have $215,637.05	Sister 2 will have $287,203.17
After 40 years, assuming the same rate of return?	Sister 1 will have $302,866.34	Sister 2 will have $420,240.29
After 45 years, assuming the same rate of return?	Sister 1 will have $425,381.54	Sister 2 will have $614,902.36

year for the next five years, an investor paying "just" 0.97 percent is giving away nearly 20 percent of her profits every year.

It's hard to imagine that, over 45 years, the true cost of such "small fees" can amount to more than a $180,000 difference on just a $20,000 investment. Costs matter, and you don't want the industry to fool you with small percentages.

Singapore residents embrace their indexing journey

Seng Su Lin and Gordon Cyr met in 2001 while volunteering at the Special Olympics in Singapore. Gordon teaches at Singapore American School and Seng Su Lin (who goes by Su) teaches technical writing at Singapore Polytechnic and at the National University of Singapore, while busily pursuing her PhD in psycholinguistics, the study of how humans acquire and use language.

The couple married in 2008, and Gordon (originally from Canada) looked over his investments with frustration. He explained his concerns:

"I used to teach in Kenya, and the school mandated that we invest our money with one of two companies. One of them was an offshore investment company called Zurich International Life Limited, <www.zurich.com/international/singapore/home/welcome.htm> headquartered on the Isle of Man. They invested in actively managed funds, but I started to feel cheated. Before opening the account, I clearly asked the representative if I could have control of how much or how little I was investing, and he said that I could. But after some time had passed, I wanted to stop contributing. The statements were really confusing. I couldn't see how much I had deposited over time and it was tough to see what my account was even worth."[13]

Feeling uncomfortable, Gordon thought it would be easy to stop making his monthly payments to the company. But the Zurich representative (who no longer works for the firm) said Gordon had signed a contract to deposit a certain amount each month—and that he had to stick to it. Frustrated, Gordon pulled his money from Zurich, and was levied a heavy penalty for doing so.

Keen to take control of his money, Gordon opened an account with DBS Vickers <www.dbsvickers.com/Pages/default.aspx> in Singapore, to create a balanced, diversified account of Exchange

Traded Index Funds similar to the "couch potato" formula that Keith Wakelin (our previously profiled Canadian) was following. The main difference was that Gordon didn't know where he and Su would eventually retire.

Su's family is in Singapore, Gordon's family is in Canada, and they own a piece of land in Hawaii. For that reason, Gordon thought it would be prudent to split his assets between Singaporean, Canadian and other global stock and bond markets. Here's what their portfolio of Exchange Traded Fund indexes looks like:

- 20 percent in the Singapore Bond index (Ticker Symbol A35)

- 20 percent in Singapore's Stock Market Index (Ticker Symbol ES3)

- 20 percent in Canada's Short-Term Bond Index (Ticker Symbol XSB)

- 20 percent in Canada's Stock Market Index (Ticker Symbol XIC)

- 20 percent in the World Stock Market Index (Ticker Symbol VT)

The first two indexes above trade on the Singaporean Stock Market; the following two trade on the Canadian Stock Exchange; and the last one, the World Stock Market Index, trades on the New York Stock Exchange. But you can purchase them all online using Singaporean brokerage firm DBS Vickers.

Gordon and Su rebalance their account with new purchases every month. For example, if the Singapore Bond Index hasn't done as well as the others, after a month it will represent less than 20 percent of their total investment. (Remember that they've allocated 20 percent of their account for each of the five indexes.) So when they add fresh money to their account, they would add to the Singapore Index. If the World Stock Index, the Canadian Stock Index, and the Singapore Stock Index have increased, leaving Gordon and Su with less than 40 percent in their combined bond indexes, then they would add fresh money to the bond indexes when making their next investment.

This ensures a couple of things:

- They're rebalancing their portfolio to increase its overall safety.

- They're buying the laggards, which over the long term will likely ensure higher returns.

If you are interested in following step by step instructions on how to buy Exchange Traded Index Funds in Singapore, you can access my website at the following: <http://andrewhallam.com/2010/10/singaporeans-investing-cheaply-with-exchange-traded-index-funds/>.

More Singaporeans are catching on

Always remember that the financial service industry's goal is to make money—for them, not for you. Not to miss the boat, Singaporeans are catching on to the benefits of low-cost investing.

Financial blogger Kay Toh, at Moneytalk.sg, compared the Singapore Straits Times Index Exchange Traded Fund performance (May 6, 2004 to May 6, 2009) with the Singapore stock market unit trusts available through Fundsupermart. You can see the results of each of the funds in Table 6.8.

Table 6.8 Singapore Market Unit Trust Performances vs. Singapore Stock Market Index (May 6, 2004 to May 6, 2009)

As of May 6, 2009	Annualized Returns over Five Years
UOB United Growth Fund	2.16%
Schroder Singapore Trust CL A	2.21%
SGAM Singapore Dividend Growth	6.1%
Lion Global Singapore Trust	3.18%
HGIF Singapore Eq-A USD	−2.23%
DWS Singapore Equity Fund	6.36%
DBS Shenton Thrift	−0.03%
Aberdeen Singapore Equity	5.42%
The returns for the above funds include the effects of reinvested dividends	
Singapore Straits Times Index Exchange Traded Fund, including dividends	7.66%

Sources: Fundsupermart, Singapore Exchange, Streetracks[14]

Will some of the unit trusts have years where they beat the market index? Absolutely, but you don't know which ones will dominate and no one else does either.

Considering that no one can pick which unit trusts (actively managed funds) might outperform the indexes in the future, the educated investor doesn't bother with the gamble and follows Su and Gordon's lead: building portfolios with low-cost indexes.

Indexing in Australia—Winning with an American Weapon

Twenty-eight-year-old Australian, Neerav Bhatt, makes his living doing something few people could have imagined possible just a decade ago. He's a full-time blogger. Sitting behind a computer screen for most of the day, Neerav says he does a lot more reading than writing. Constantly on the lookout for inspiration, he devours online articles to spark his creative energy, often giving him something to comment on for his own blog.

His prolific reading exposed him to the superiority of index funds over actively managed mutual funds (known as unit trusts in Australia). "Most financial advisers are just salespeople. And people are far too trusting of them," he says, explaining that most Australians just wander into a bank and buy their investment products, which generally charge nearly two percent a year in fees.

After first reading a newspaper article on index funds, Neerav investigated further by studying a copy of Princeton University Professor Burton Malkiel's classic book, A *Random Walk Down Wall Street*. Then, he discovered the American nonprofit investment company Vanguard, which had set up shop in his native Australia.

"Vanguard had been around for ages in Australia, but nobody was talking about it," he said. And Neerav recognized why. Most people get their financial knowledge and education from advisers who make their living selling high-cost products. Vanguard's the thorn in the side of an investment-service community that wants to keep reaping as many fees as possible from unsuspecting investors.

Neerav discovered that Australians can open accounts with Vanguard and they can usually transfer their superannuation to Vanguard as well.[15] Vanguard offers individual indexes for the Australian markets and the international markets, but one of the more cost-effective ways of investing with Vanguard Australia is with its Life Strategy Funds. They're combinations of indexes, complete portfolios in a single fund, and the fee structure decreases as the account swells in value.

Alternatively, if they built a portfolio of separate index funds through Vanguard Australia, they could feasibly end up paying much higher overall fees. That's because the fee structure is determined on the size of each fund, not on the size of each account. The more money an investor has in each fund, the lower the percentage fee. So an investor with $200,000 could pay a lot less with a Vanguard Australian Life Strategy Fund than he or she would by building a portfolio with separate Vanguard indexes. Table 6.9 reveals the relative costs.

The fund you choose will depend on your tolerance for risk. If you're interested in an allocation of bonds that's close to your age, then you could choose from the following respective funds.

1. Vanguard Life Strategy High Growth Fund: <www.vanguard .com.au/personal_investors/investment/managed-funds-up-to-$500000/diversified/high-growth.cfm> 10 percent bonds,

Table **6.9** Vanguard Australia's Life Strategy Fund Options (Quoted in Australian dollars)

Life Strategy Index Funds	Allocation	Fees Based on Account Size
Vanguard Life Strategy Conservative Fund	70% bond indexes and cash 30% Australian and International stock indexes	0.9% on the first $50,000 0.6% on the next $50,000 0.35% on the balance above $100,000
Vanguard Life Strategy Balanced Fund	50% bond indexes and cash 50% Australian and International stock indexes	0.9% on the first $50,000 0.6% on the next $50,000 0.35% on the balance above $100,000
Vanguard Life Strategy Growth Fund	30% bond indexes and cash 70% Australian and International stock indexes	0.9% on the first $50,000 0.6% on the next $50,000 0.35% on the balance above $100,000
Vanguard Life Strategy High Growth Fund	10% bond indexes and cash 90% Australian and International stock indexes	0.9% on the first $50,000 0.6% on the next $50,000 0.35% on the balance above $100,000

Source: Vanguard Investments Australia[16]

90 percent stocks. This is well suited for high-risk investors or investors in their late teens or 20s.

2. Vanguard Life Strategy Growth Fund: <www.vanguard.com .au/personal_investors/investment/managed-funds-up-to-$500000/diversified/growth.cfm> 30 percent bonds, 70 percent stocks. This benefits investors in their 30s and 40s.

3. Vanguard Life Strategy Balanced Fund: <www.vanguard .com.au/personal_investors/investment/managed-funds-up-to-$500000/diversified/balanced.cfm> 50 percent bonds, 50 percent stocks. Conservative younger investors or investors in their 50s and 60s might prefer the conservative nature of this fund, which still has capacity for growth with 50 percent allocated to stock indexes.

4. Vanguard Life Strategy Conservative Fund: <www.vanguard .com.au/personal_investors/investment/managed-funds-up-to-$500000/diversified/conservative.cfm> 70 percent bonds, 30 percent stocks. Retirees or extremely conservative investors might find this fund to be the right fit.[17]

Another word about risk

Investors with a corporate or government pension might not feel the need to invest so conservatively. For example, a 50-year-old school teacher with a pension might prefer to buy the Growth Fund instead of the Conservative Fund. Over time, the Growth Fund will likely do better, but the volatility will be higher. If someone has a strong alternative source of retirement income, then they might want to take a higher risk/higher return option.

Neerav might be right when suggesting that most Australians are unaware of Vanguard. But one thing's for sure, there is economy in numbers. The more Australians who catch onto Vanguard, the cheaper its products will become.

The Next Step

Once you learn how to build indexed accounts, the time commitment you will spend on making investment decisions and transactions will be minimal. You could end up spending less than one hour a year on your investments.

Nobody is going to know how the stock and bond markets will perform over the next 5, 10, 20 or 30 years. But one thing is certain: if you build a diversified account of index funds, you'll beat 90 percent of professional investors. In a taxable account, you'll do even better.

There's only one risk standing in the way of your investment success, and it's an ironic one. If you speak to an adviser at a financial institution, they will do their best to convince you to follow a higher-cost, less-effective option. In my next chapter, I'll reveal some of the tricks they use to keep investors away from index funds.

Notes

1. Morningstar.com, Rebalanced fund returns for Vanguard's U.S. total stock market index (VTSMX), Vanguard's international stock market index (VGTSX), and Vanguard's total bond market index (VBMFX) (2006–2011).
2. Morningstar.com, Fund returns for Fidelity Balanced (FBALX), T Rowe Price Balanced (RPBAX), and American Funds Balanced (ABALX) (2006–2011).
3. Morningstar.com, fund turnover rates.
4. Morningstar.com, fund turnover rates for Vanguard's Target Retirement Funds.
5. "Global Couch Potato Performance," accessed January 10, 2011, http://www.canadianbusiness.com/my_money/investing/article.jsp?content=20070123_122259_5192&ref=related.
6. Globeinvestor.com Fund Performances.
7. Toronto Dominion Bank, e-Series index funds, accessed April 15, 2011, http://www.tdcanadatrust.com/mutualfunds/tdeseriesfunds/index.jsp.
8. Ibid.
9. Ajay Khorana, Henri Servaes, and Peter Tufano, "Mutual Fund Fees Around the World," *The Review of Financial Studies* 2008 Vol. 22, No. 3 (Oxford University Press) accessed April 15, 2011, http://faculty.london.edu/hservaes/rfs2009.pdf.
10. Toronto Dominion Bank, e-Series index funds, accessed April 15, 2011, http://www.tdcanadatrust.com/mutualfunds/tdeseriesfunds/index.jsp.

11. Infinity S&P 500 Index Fund Costs, accessed January 10, 2011, http://www.fundsupermart.com/main/fundinfo/viewFund.svdo? sedolnumber=370283#charge.

12. Vanguard S&P 500 Exchange Traded Fund Cost, accessed January 10, 2011, http://finance.yahoo.com/q/pr?s=SPY+Profile.

13. Personal Interview with Gordon Cyr, October 18, 2010, in Singapore.

14. Fundsupermart.com for actively managed Singapore market unit trust performances, accessed May 2009, http://www.fund supermart.com/main/home/index.svdo; Singapore exchange traded fund historical prices, accessed May 2009, www.sgx .com; Historical dividends for Singapore market ETF: Streetracks .com, accessed May 2009, http://www.streettracks.com.sg/ssga/ jsp/en/AnnualReport.jsp.

15. Vanguard Australia, Life Strategy Funds and Fees, accessed November 1, 2010, http://www.vanguard.com.au/personal_ investors/investment/managed-funds-up-to-$500000/diversified/ diversified_home.cfm.

16. Ibid.

17. Ibid.

Peek Inside A Pilferer's Playbook

If you've read what I've written so far about indexed investing, I hope that you're planning to open your own indexed account. Or perhaps you'll want to find a fee-only adviser who can set it up for you.

Either way, if you currently have a financial adviser buying you actively managed mutual funds, you're probably thinking of making the split.

That might be easier said than done. I like to think that the majority of investors who have attended my seminars have decided to index their investments—to save costs and taxes—while building larger accounts than they would have done with baskets of less-efficient products. But not all have. I know many would-be indexers spoke to their financial advisers, fully intending to break free, but the advisers' sales pitch froze them in their tracks.

Many financial advisers have mental playbooks designed to deter would-be index investors and they initiate their strategies with remarkable success, metaphorically ensuring that their clients continue climbing Mount Kilimanjaro with 50-pound packs on their backs.

How Will Most Financial Advisers Fight You?

Often, when a friend or family member wants to open an investment account, he or she asks me to come along. Beforehand, I briefly talk to the new investor about the markets, how they work, and the merits of index investing. I tell the person that every single academic study done on mutual fund investing points to the same conclusion: to give yourself the best possible odds in the stock market, low-cost index funds are key.

Walking into a bank or financial service company, we're then settled into plush chairs across from a financial adviser selling us on the merits of his ability to choose actively managed mutual funds. When my friend brings up the merits of index funds, the salesperson has an arsenal of anti-index sales talk.

Here are some of the rebuttals the advisers will give you— desperate, of course, to keep money flowing into their pockets and the firm's. If you're prepared for what they might say, you'll have a better chance of standing your ground. Don't forget. It's your money, not theirs.

Index funds are dangerous when stock markets fall. Active fund managers never keep all their eggs in the stock market in case it drops. A stock market index is linked 100 percent to the stock market's return.

This is where a salesperson pushes a client's fear button— suggesting that active managers have the ability to quickly sell stock market assets before the markets drop, saving your mutual fund assets from falling too far during a crash. And then, when the markets are looking "safer" (or so the pitch goes), a mutual fund manager will then buy stocks again, allowing you to ride the wave of profits back as the stock market recovers.

It all sounds good in sales theory, but they can't time the market like that—and hidden fees still take their toll. Ask your adviser to tell you which calendar year in recent memory saw the biggest decline. He should say 2008. Ask him if most actively managed funds beat the total stock market index during 2008. If he says yes, then you've caught him talking out the side of his head. A Standard & Poor's study cited in *The Wall Street Journal* in 2009, detailed the truth: The vast majority of actively managed funds still lost to their counterpart stock market indexes during 2008—the worst market drop in recent memory.[1] Clearly, actively managed fund managers weren't able to dive out of the markets on time.

What's more, a single stock market index is just part of a port- folio. Don't let an adviser fool you with data comparing a single index fund with the actively managed products they're selling. As you read in Chapter 5, smart investors balance their portfolios with bond indexes as well.

You can't beat the market with an index fund, they'll say. An index fund will give you just an average return. Why saddle yourself with mediocrity when we have teams of people to select the best funds for you?

I've heard this from a number of advisers. And it makes me smile. If the average mutual fund had no costs associated with it— no 12B1 fee, no expense ratio, no taxable liability, no sales commissions or adviser trailer fees, and no operational costs—then the salesperson would be right. A total stock market index fund's return would be pretty close to "average." Long term, roughly half of the world's actively managed funds would beat the world stock market index, and roughly half of the world's funds would be beaten by it. But for that to happen, you would have to live in the following fantasy world:

1. Your adviser would have to work for free. No trailer fees or sales commissions for him/her or the firm. The tooth fairy would pay his mortgage, food bills, vacations, and other worldly expenses.

2. The fund company wouldn't make any money. Companies such as Raymond James, T. Rowe Price, Fidelity, Putnam Investments, Goldman Sachs, (and the rest of the "for-profit" wealth-management businesses) would be charitable foundations.

3. The researchers would work for free. Not only would the fund companies bless the world with their services, but also their ranks of researchers would be altruistic, independently wealthy philanthropists giving their time and efforts to humanity.

4. The fund managers doing the buying and selling for the mutual funds would work for free. They would be so inspired by their parent companies that they would trade stocks and bonds for free while lesser-evolved mortals worked for salaries.

5. **The fund companies could trade stocks for free.** Large brokerage firms would take the financial hit for the trading done by mutual fund companies. Recognizing the fund companies "value-added" mission, brokerage firms would pay every commission a fund company racked up from trading stocks.

6. **Governments would waive your taxable obligations.** Because the fund companies are such a blessing on the world, the world's governments would turn a blind eye to the taxable turnover established.

If the fantasy scenario above were correct, then yes, a total stock market index fund would generate very close to an average return.

But in the real world, advisers suggesting that a total stock market index gives an average return are proving to be well-dressed Pinocchios or post-Columbus sailors with a "Flat Earth" complex.

But a tough salesperson wouldn't give up there. Next, you might hear something like this:

I can show you plenty of mutual funds that have beaten the indexes. We'd only buy you the very best funds.

It's pretty easy to look in the rearview mirror at the last 15 winners of Golf's British Open Championship and say: "See, here are the champions who won the British Open over the past 15 years. These are people who can win. This knowledge qualifies me to pick the next 15 years' worth of champions—and we'll bet your money on my selections."

Studies prove that high-performing funds of the past rarely continue their outperforming ways.

Just look at the system used by Morningstar's mutual fund rating system. No one in the world has more mutual fund data than Morningstar. Certainly, your local financial adviser doesn't. But as detailed in Chapter 3, the funds given "top scores" by Morningstar for their superb, consistent performance usually go on to lose to the market indexes in the following years.

Even Morningstar recognizes the incongruity. John Rekenthaler, director of research, said in the fall 2000 edition of *In The Vanguard*:

"To be fair, I don't think that you'd want to pay much attention to Morningstar's ratings either."[2]

So if Morningstar can't pick the top mutual funds of the future, what odds does your financial planner have—especially when trying to dazzle you with a fund's historical track record?

If you're the kind of person who enjoys winding people up, try this comeback out the next time an adviser tries selling you (or one of your friends) on a bunch of funds that he claims have beaten the index over the past 15 years.

Hey, that's great. They all beat the index over the past 15 years. Now show me your personal investment account statements from 15 years ago. If you can show me that you owned all of these funds back then, I'll invest every penny I have with you.

OK—maybe that's a bit mean. You aren't likely to see any of those funds in his 15-year-old portfolio reports.

If the salesperson deserves an "A" for tenacity, you'll get this as the next response:

But I'm a professional. I can bounce your money around from fund to fund, taking advantage of global economic swings and hot fund manager streaks and easily beat a portfolio of diversified indexes.

Just thinking about that kind of love gives me goose bumps. Many advisers will lead you to believe that they have their pulse on the economy—that they can foresee opportunities and pending disasters. Their sagacity, they will suggest, will enable you to beat a portfolio of indexes.

But in terms of financial acumen, brokers and financial advisers are at the bottom of the totem pole. At the top, you have pension fund managers, mutual fund managers, and hedge fund managers. Most financial advisers, as U.S. personal finance commentator Suze Orman points out, are "just pin-striped suited salespeople."

Your financial planner could have just a two-week course under her belt. At best, a certified financial planner needs just one year of sales experience at a brokerage firm, and fewer than six months of full-time academic training (on investment products, insurance, and financial planning), before receiving his or her certification With some regular nightly reading, it wouldn't take long before you knew more about personal finance than most financial planners. They have to sell. They have to build trust. They have to make you feel good about yourself. These skills are the biggest part of their jobs.

When arbitration lawyer Daniel Solin was writing his book, *Does Your Broker Owe You Money?*, a broker told him:

> *Training for a new broker goes something like this: Study and take the Series 7, 63, 65 and insurance exams. I spent three weeks learning to sell. If a broker wants to learn about (asset allocation and diversification) it has to be done on the broker's own time.*[3]

This might explain why it's often common to find investors of all ages without any bonds in their portfolios. Predominantly trained as salespeople, it's possible that many financial representatives aren't schooled in the practice of diversifying investment accounts with stocks and bonds.

Noted U.S. finance writer William Bernstein echoes the gaps in most financial adviser training, suggesting in his superb 2002 book, *The Four Pillars of Investing*, that anyone who invests money should read the two classic texts:

1. *A Random Walk Down Wall Street* by Burton Malkiel

2. *Common Sense on Mutual Funds* by John Bogle

"After you're finished with these two books, you will know more about finance than 99 percent of all stockbrokers and most other finance professionals," he said.[4]

From what I've seen, he's right.

When my good friend Dave Alfawicki and I went into a bank in White Rock, British Columbia, in 2004, we met a young woman selling mutual funds. Dave wanted to set up an indexed account, and I went along for the ride. The adviser's knowledge gaps were extraordinary, so I asked the question: What kinds of certification do you have and how long did it take? She received her license to sell mutual funds through a course called Investment Funds in

Canada (IFIC). It's supposed to take three weeks of full-time studying to complete the course, but she and her classmates finished it in just two intensive weeks.[5] Before the two-week course, she knew nothing about investing.

A year later, I went into another Canadian bank with my mom to help her open an investment account. We wanted the account to have roughly 50 percent in a stock index and 50 percent in a bond index. Of course, the adviser, as usual, tried talking us out of it.

But once the adviser recognized that I knew more about investing than she did, she came clean. To paraphrase the discussion, she shocked us with this:

First, we get a feel for the client. The bank suggests that if the client doesn't know much about investing, we should put them in a fund of funds, for example, a mutual fund that would have a series of funds within it. It tends to be a bit more expensive than regular mutual funds. This sales job only works with investors who really don't know what they're doing.

If the investor seems a little smarter, we offer them, individually, our in-house brand of actively managed mutual funds. We don't make as much money with these, so we push for the other products first.

Under no circumstances do we offer the bank's index funds to clients. If an investor requests them and we can't talk them out of the indexes, only then will we buy them for the client.

I appreciated her candor. By the end of the conversation, the adviser was asking me for book suggestions about indexed investing and she gratefully wrote down a number of titles. At least she was willing to take care of her personal portfolio.

Three years later, a different representative from the same bank phoned my mom. "Your account is too risky," he said. "Come on down to the bank so we can move some things around for you."

Thankfully, my mom was able to stand her ground. With 50 percent of her investment in bond indexes, the account wasn't risky at all—but it wasn't profitable for the bank.

If you notice a financial adviser has a university degree in finance, commerce, or business, hang tight for a moment. Find someone else with one of these degrees and ask this: During your studies at university, did you study mutual funds, index funds, or learn how to build a personal investment portfolio for wealth building or retirement? The answer will paradoxically be no. So don't be fooled by an additional, irrelevant title.

Most brokers and advisers really are just salespeople, and well-paid salespeople at that. In the U.S., the average broker makes nearly $150,000 a year—putting them in the top five percent of all U.S. wage earners. They make more than the average lawyer, primary care doctor, or professor at an elite university.[6] And if they're recommending actively managed funds, they're a bit like vendors in the guise of nutritionists selling candy, booze, and cigarettes.

The Totem Pole View

Financial advisers and brokers are at the bottom of the totem pole of financial knowledge. At the top, you'll find hedge fund managers, mutual fund managers, and pension fund managers.

Generally earning the highest certification in money management— as certified financial analysts—pension fund managers have the leeway to buy what they want. These are the folks managing huge sums of government and corporate retirement money. Arguably, they're the best of the best. If your local financial planner applied for the job of managing the pension for Pennsylvania's teachers or New Jersey's state-pension system, he or she would likely get laughed off the table.

Pension fund managers have their pulses on the stock markets and the economy. They can invest where they want. Typically, they don't have to focus on a particular geographic region or type of stock. The world is their oyster. If they want to jump into European stocks, they do it. If they think the new opportunities are in small stocks, they load up on those. If they feel the stock market is going to take a short-term beating, they might sell off some of their stocks, buying more bonds or holding cash instead.

Your typical financial planner isn't as knowledgeable as the average pension fund manager. But most advisers will try and "sell" you on the idea that (like the pension fund manager) they have their pulse on the economy and that they can find you hot mutual funds to buy. They might try telling you that they know when the economy is going to self-destruct, which stock market is going to fly, and whether gold, silver, small stocks, large stocks, oil stocks, or retail stocks are going to do well this quarter, this year, or this decade.

But they are full of hot air.

Pension fund managers are more likely to know oodles more about making money in the markets than financial advisers or brokers.

Knowing that pension fund managers are like the gods of the industry, how do their results stack up against a diversified portfolio of index funds?

Most pension funds have their money in a 60/40 split: 60 percent stocks and 40 percent bonds. They also have advantages that retail investors don't have: large company pension funds pay significantly lower fees than retail investors like you or I would, and they don't have to pay taxes on capital gains that are incurred.

Considering the financial acumen of the average pension fund manager, coupled with the lower cost and tax benefits, you would assume that the average American pension fund would easily beat an indexed portfolio allocated similarly to most pension funds: 60 percent stocks and 40 percent bonds. But that isn't the case.

U.S. consulting firm, FutureMetrics, studied the performance of 192 U.S. major corporate pension plans between 1988 and 2005. Fewer than 30 percent of the pension funds outperformed a portfolio of 60 percent S&P 500 index and 40 percent intermediate corporate bond index.[7]

If most pension fund managers can't beat an indexed portfolio, what chance does your financial planner have?

The best odds to win

If you told most financial advisers this, they would either begin talking in circles to confuse you, or they would desperately be battling with their ego.

If it's the latter, you might hear this: If it were so easy, why wouldn't every pension fund be indexed?

Pension fund managers are as optimistic as the rest of us. Many of them will try to beat portfolios comprised of a 60 percent stock index and a 40 percent bond index.

But they aren't stupid, and many pension funds maximize their returns by indexing.

According to U.S. financial adviser Bill Schultheis, author of *The New Coffeehouse Investor*, the Washington state pension fund, for example, has 100 percent of its stock market assets in indexes, California has 86 percent indexed, New York has 75 percent indexed, and Connecticut has 84 percent of its stock market money in indexes.[8]

The vast majority of regular, everyday investors, however, (about 95 percent of individual investors) buy actively managed mutual funds instead.[9] Unaware of the data, their financial advisers distort realities to keep their gravy trains flowing. It will cost most people more than half of their retirement portfolios—thanks to fees, taxes, and dumb "market timing" mistakes.

Sticking with index funds might be boring. But it beats winding up as shark bait, and it gives you the best odds of eventually growing rich through the stock and bond markets.

Is Government Action Required?

David Swensen, Yale University's endowment fund manager, suggests the U.S. government needs to stop the mutual fund industry's exploitation of individual investors.[10] The U.S. has some of the lowest cost actively managed funds in the world. I wonder what he would think of Canada's costs, Great Britain's costs, or Singapore's costs, all of which are significantly higher.

You can't wait for government regulation. The best weapon against exploitation is education. You might not have learned this in high school, but you're learning it now.

Among those hearing the call to arms and taking action to educate others is Google's vice president, Jonathan Rosenberg.

In August 2004, Google shares <www.google.com/intl/en/about/corporate/company> became available on public stock exchanges and many Google employees (who already held Google shares privately) became overnight millionaires when the stock price soared.

The waves of cascading wealth on Google's employees attracted streams of financial planners from firms such as JPMorgan Chase <www.jpmorgan.com>, UBS <www.ubs.com>, Morgan Stanley <www.morganstanley.com>, and Presidio Financial Partners <www.thepresidiogroupllc.com>. Drawn like sharks to blood, they circled Google, wanting to enter the company's headquarters so they could sell actively managed mutual funds to the newly rich employees.

Google's top brass put the financial planners on hold. Employees were then presented with a series of guest lecturers before the financial planners were allowed on company turf.

According to Mark Dowie who wrote about the story for *San Francisco* magazine in 2008, the first to arrive was Stanford University's William Sharpe, the 1990 Nobel laureate economist. He advised the staff to avoid actively managed mutual funds: "Don't try to beat the market. Put your money in some indexed mutual funds."[11]

A week later, Burton Malkiel arrived. The professor of economics at Princeton University urged the employees to build portfolios of index funds. He has been studying mutual fund investing since the early 1970s, and he vehemently believes it's not possible to choose actively managed funds that will beat a total stock market index over the long term. Don't believe anyone (a broker, adviser, friend, or magazine) suggesting otherwise.

Next, the staff was fortunate enough to hear John Bogle speak. A champion for the "little guy," John Bogle is the financial genius who founded the nonprofit investment group, Vanguard. His message was the same: The brokers and financial advisers swimming around Google's massive raft have a single purpose. They're a giant fleecing machine wanting to take your money through high fees— and you may not realize what is happening until it's too late.

When the sharks finally approached the raft, staff members at Google were armed to the teeth, easily fending off the well-dressed, well-spoken, charming advisers.[12]

I hope that you'll be able to do the same as the crew at Google. But don't forget that for most financial advisers, index funds are pariahs. If you have an adviser today, and you're not invested in index funds, then you already know (based on their absence in your portfolio) that your adviser has a conflict of interest. In that case, asking your adviser how he feels about indexes is going to be a waste of time.

After one of my seminars on index funds, I often hear someone say: "I'm going to ask my adviser about index funds." That's like asking the owner of a McDonald's restaurant to tell you all about Burger King. They won't want you stepping anywhere near the Whopper.

And they certainly won't want you paying attention to the leader of Harvard University's Endowment Fund, Jack Meyer. When interviewed by William C. Symonds in 2004 for *Bloomberg Businessweek*, he said:

> *"The investment business is a giant scam. It deletes billions of dollars every year in transaction costs and fees... Most people think they can find fund managers who can outperform, but most people are wrong. You should simply hold index funds. No doubt about it"*[13]

Clearly, investing in index funds is a way to statistically ensure the highest odds of investment success. Doing so, however, means that you will need to stand your ground and perhaps take the road less traveled, while most people succumb to the impressive sales rhetoric that leads them toward—at the very least—investment mediocrity with actively managed mutual funds. If you want to grow rich on an average salary, you can't afford to invest in the expensive products sold by most financial advisers.

A huge risk, however, is when investors start looking at options to enhance their investment returns even further than what an indexed portfolio would provide. The following chapter outlines some common mistakes that people make, with a strong message to avoid the same mistakes yourself.

Notes

1. Sam Mamudi, "Indexing Wins Again," *The Wall Street Journal*, April 23, 2009.

2. An interview with Morningstar research director John Rekenthaler, *In the Vanguard*, Fall 2000, accessed April 18, 2011, http://www.vanguard.com/pdf/itvautumn2000.pdf.

3. Daniel Solin, *The Smartest Investment Book You'll Ever Read* (New York: Penguin, 2006), 48.

4. William Bernstein, *The Four Pillars of Investing, Lessons for Building a Winning Portfolio* (New York: McGraw Hill, 2002), 224.

5. Investment Funds in Canada Course (IFIC), accessed April 15, 2011, http://db2.centennialcollege.ca/ce/coursedetail.php?Course Code=CCSC-103.

6. Daniel Solin, *The Smartest Investment Book You'll Ever Read*, 79.

7. Larry Swedroe, *The Quest For Alpha* (Hoboken, New Jersey: John Wiley & Sons, 2011), 133–134.

8. Bill Schultheis, *The New Coffeehouse Investor, How to Build Wealth, Ignore Wall Street, And Get On With Your Life* (New York: Penguin, 2009), 51–52.

9. Paul Farrell, *The Lazy Person's Guide to Investing* (New York: Warner Business Books, 2004), xxii.

10. David F. Swensen, *Unconventional Success, a Fundamental Approach to Personal Investment*, (New York: Free Press, 2005), 1.

11. Mark Dowie, "The Best Investment Advice You'll Never Get," San Francisco Magazine Online, accessed November 6, 2010, http://www.sanfranmag.com/story/best-investment-advice-youll -never-get.

12. Ibid.

13. William C. Symonds, "Husbanding that $27 Billion (extended)," December 27, 2004, accessed April 15, 2011, http://www.business week.com/magazine/content/04_52/b3914474.htm.

Avoid Seduction

The trouble with taking charge of your own finances is the risk of falling for some kind of scam. Learning how to beat the vast majority of professional investors is easy: invest in index funds. But some people make the mistake of branching off to experiment with alternative investments.

Achieving success with a new financial strategy can be one of the worst things to happen. If something works out over a one-, three- or five-year period, there's going to be a temptation to do it again, to take another risk. But it's important to control the seductive temptation of seemingly easy money. There's a world of hurt out there and rascals keen to separate you from your hard-earned savings. In this chapter, I'll examine some of the seductive strategies used by marketers out for a quick buck. With luck, you'll avoid them.

Confession Time

Perhaps I'm justifying this to feel better about myself, but this is what I believe: Any investor who doesn't have a story relating to a really dumb investment decision is probably a liar. So I'm going to roll up my sleeves and tell you about the dumbest investment decision I ever made. It might prevent you from making a similar, silly mistake.

The dumbest investment I ever made

In 1998, a friend of mine asked me if I would be interested in investing in a company called Insta-Cash Loans. "They pay 54 percent annually in interest," he whispered. "And I know a few guys who are already invested and collecting interest payments."

For any half-witted investor, the high interest rate should have raised red flags. Around that time, I was reading about the danger of high-paying corporate bonds issued by companies such as WorldCom, which was yielding 8.3 percent. The gist of the warning was this: If a company is paying 8.3 percent interest on a bond in a climate where four percent is the norm, then there has to be a troublesome fire burning in the basement. Not long after WorldCom issued its bonds, the company declared bankruptcy. It was borrowing money from banks to pay its bond interest.[1]

The 54 percent annual return that my friend's investment prospect paid was a Mt. Everest of interest compared with Worldcom's speed bump. It rightfully scared me to think of how crazy the investment venture must be, telling my friend as much:

"Look," I said, "Insta-Cash Loans isn't really paying you 54 percent interest. If you give the company $10,000, and the company pays out $5,400 at the end of the year in 'interest,' you've only received slightly more than half of your investment back. If that guy disappears into the Malaysian foothills with that $10,000, you get the shaft. You'd lose $4,600."

It seemed totally crazy. But what's even crazier is that I eventually changed my mind.

After the first year, my friend told me that he had received his 54 percent interest payment. "No you didn't," I insisted. "Your original money could still vaporize."

The following year, he received 54 percent in interest again, paid out regularly with 4.5 percent monthly deposits into his bank account.

Although I still thought it was a scam, my conviction was losing steam. It appeared that now he was ahead of the game, receiving more in interest than he had given the company in the first place.

He increased his investment to $80,000 in Insta-Cash Loans, which paid him $43,200 annually in "interest."

As a retiree, he was able to travel all over the world on these interest payments. He went to Argentina, Thailand, Laos, and Hawaii— all on the back of this fabulous investment.

After about five years, he convinced me to meet the head of this company, Daryl Klein (and yes, that's his real name). How was Insta-Cash Loans able to pay out 54 percent in interest every year to each of its investors? I wanted to know how the business worked.

I drove to the company's headquarters in Nanaimo, British Columbia, with a friend who was also intrigued.

Pulling alongside the curb in front of Daryl's office, I was skeptical. Daryl was standing on the sidewalk in a creased shirt with his sleeves rolled up, a cigarette in hand.

We settled into Daryl's office and he explained the business. Initially, he had intended to open a pawn brokerage but changed his mind when he caught on to the far-more lucrative business of loaning money and taking cars as collateral. As a result, Insta-Cash Loans was created.

In a narrative recreation, this is what he said:

I loan small amounts of short-term money to people who wouldn't ordinarily be able to get loans. For example, if a real estate agent sells a house and knows he has a big commission coming and he wants to buy a new stereo right away, he can come to me if his credit cards are maxed out and if he doesn't have the cash for the stereo.

"How does that work?" I wanted to know.

Well, if he owns a car outright, and he turns the ownership over to me, I'll loan him the money. The car is just collateral. He can keep driving it, but I own it. I charge him a high-interest rate, plus a pawn fee, and if he defaults on the loan, I can legally take the car. When he repays the loan, I give the car's ownership back.

"What if they just take off with the car?" I asked.

I have some great retired ladies working for me who are fabulous at tracking down these cars. One guy drove straight across the country when he defaulted on the loan. One of these ladies found out that he was in Ontario (about a six-hour flight from Daryl's office in British Columbia) and before the guy even knew it, we had that car on the next train for British Columbia. In the end, we handed him the bill for the loan interest, plus the freight cost for his car.

It sounded like a pretty efficient operation to me. But I wanted to know if the guy had a heart. "Hey Daryl," I asked, "have you ever forgiven anyone who didn't pay up?"

Leaning back in his chair with a self-satisfied smile, Daryl told the story of a woman who borrowed money from him, using the family motor home as collateral. She defaulted on the loan, but she didn't think it was fair that Daryl should be able to keep the motor home. Her husband had not known about the loan. He came into Daryl's office with a lawyer, but the contract was legally airtight; there was nothing the lawyer could do about it.

But, as Daryl explained, he took pity on the woman and gave the motor-home ownership back to the couple.

It sounded like an amazing operation.

However, nobody can guarantee you 54 percent on your money—ever. Bernie Madoff, the currently incarcerated Ponzi-scheming money manager in the U.S. promised a minimum return of 10 percent annually and he sucked scores of intelligent people into his self-servicing vacuum cleaner—absconding with $65 billion in the process.[2] He claimed to be making money for his clients by investing their cash mostly in the stock market, but he just paid them "interest" with new investors' deposits. The account balances that his clients saw weren't real. When an investor wanted to withdraw money, Madoff took the proceeds from fresh money that was deposited by other investors.

When the floor finally fell out from underneath Madoff during the 2008 financial crisis, investors lost everything. His victims included actors Kevin Bacon, his wife Kyra Sedgwick, and director Steven Spielberg, among the many others who lost millions with Madoff.[3]

Yet the percentages paid by Madoff were chicken feed compared with the 54 percent caviar reaped by Daryl Klein's investors.

Despite the solid-sounding story Daryl told me back in 2001, I still wouldn't invest money with the guy.

But my friend kept receiving his interest payments, which now exceeded $100,000.

By 2003, I had seen enough. My friend had been making money off this guy for years and my "spidey senses" were tickled more by greed than danger. I met with Daryl again, and I invested $7,000. Then I convinced an investment club that I was in to dip a toe in the water. So we did, investing $5,000. The monthly 4.5 percent interest checks were making us feel pretty smart. After a year, the investment club added another $20,000.

Other friends were also tempted by the easy money. One friend took out a loan for $50,000 and plunked it down on Insta-Cash Loans, and he began receiving $2,250 a month in interest from the company.

Another friend deposited more than $100,000 into the business; he was paid $54,000 in yearly interest. But Alice's Wonderland was more real than our fool's paradise.

Like Bernie Madoff (who was caught after Daryl) the party eventually ended in 2006 and the carnage was everywhere. We never found out whether Daryl intended for his business to be a Ponzi scheme from the beginning (he was clearly paying interest to investors from the deposits of other investors) or whether his business slowly unraveled after a well-intentioned but ineffective business plan went awry.

Klein was eventually convicted of breaching the provincial securities act, preventing him from engaging in investor-relations activities until 2026.[4]

The fact that he was slapped on the wrist, however, was small consolation for his investors. A few had even remortgaged their homes to get in on the action.

Our investment club, after collecting interest for just a few months, lost the balance of our $25,000 investment. My $7,000 personal investment also evaporated. Many investors in the company lost everything. My friend who borrowed $50,000 to invest, collected interest for 10 months (which he had to pay taxes on) before seeing his investment balance disappear when Insta-Cash Loans went bankrupt in 2006.

It's an important lesson for investors to learn. At some point in your life, someone is going to make you a lucrative promise. Give it a miss. In all likelihood, it's going to cause nothing but headaches—not to mention a potential black hole in your bank account.

Investment Newsletters and Their Track Records

In 1999, the same investment club mentioned earlier was trying to get an edge on its stock picking. We purchased an investment newsletter subscription called the *Gilder Technology Report*, <www.gildertech.com/> published by a guy named George Gilder.

Unbelievably, he is still in business. A quick online search today reveals a website that exhorts his stock picks, claiming his portfolio returned 155 percent during the past three years, and that if you buy now, you'll pay just $199 for the 12-month online subscription to his newsletter. If you're falling for that promotional garbage, I have a story for you.[5]

Back in 1999, we were convinced that George Guilder held the keys to the kingdom of wealth. Unfortunately for us, he was the king of pain. Today, if George Gilder reported his 11-year track record online (instead of trying to tempt investors with an unaudited three-year historical return) he would have a stampede of exiters. His stock picks have been abysmal for his followers.

We bought the George Gilder technology report in 1999 and we put real money down on his suggestions. I'm just hoping my investment club buddies don't read this book and learn that George Gilder is still hawking his promises of wealth. They'd probably want to send him down a river in a barrel.

Back in Chapter 4, I showed you a chart of technology companies and how far their share prices fell from 2000 to 2002.

In 2000, whose investment report recommended purchasing Nortel Networks <www.nortel.com>, Lucent Technologies <www.alcatel-lucent.com>, JDS Uniphase <www.jdsu.com> and Cisco Systems <www.cisco.com/>? You guessed it: George Gilder's.

Table 8.1 puts the reality in perspective. If you had a total of $40,000 invested in the above four "Gilder-touted" businesses in 2000, it would have dropped to $1,140 by 2002.

And how much would your investment have to gain to get back to $40,000?

Table 8.1 Prices of Technology Stocks Plummet (2000–2002)

	High Value in 2000	Low Value in 2002
Amazon.com	$10,000	$700
Cisco Systems	$10,000	$990
Corning Inc.	$10,000	$100
JDS Uniphase	$10,000	$50
Lucent Technologies	$10,000	$70
Nortel Networks	$10,000	$30
Priceline.com	$10,000	$60
Yahoo!	$10,000	$360

Source: Morningstar and Burton Malkiel's A Random Walk Guide to Investing

In percentage terms, it would need to grow 3,400 percent.

Wow—wouldn't that be a headline for the *Gilder Technology Report* today?

"Since 2002, our stock picks have made 3,400 percent"

If that really happened, George Gilder would be advertising those numbers on his site rather than showcasing a measly return of 155 percent over the past three years.

George Gilder's stock picks have tossed investors into the Grand Canyon and he's bragging that his investors have scaled back about 50 feet. He could tell the truth about his real stock-picking prowess, but then he couldn't fool newsletter subscribers looking for keys to easy wealth. There are no keys to easy wealth—so don't be fooled by advertised claims.

Just for fun, let's assume that Gilder's original stock picks from 2000 did make 3,400 percent from 2002 to 2011. That might impress a lot of people. But it wouldn't impress me. After the losses that Gilder's followers experienced from 2000 to 2002, a gain of 3,400 percent would have his long-term subscribers barely breaking even on their original investment after a decade—and that's if you didn't include the ravages of inflation.

If there are any long-term subscribers, they're nowhere near their break-even point. Can you hear his followers scrambling on the lowest slopes of the Grand Canyon? I wonder if they're thirsty.

Where there is a buck to be taken

We already know that the odds of beating a diversified portfolio of index funds, after taxes and fees, are slim. But what about investment newsletters? You can find more beautifully marketed newsletter promises than you can find people in a Tokyo subway. They selectively boast returns (like Gilder does), creating mouthwatering temptations for many inexperienced investors:

> *With our special strategy, we've made 300 percent over the past 12 months in the stock market, and now, for just*

$9.99 a month, we'll share this new wealth-building for-
mula with you!

Think about it. If somebody really could compound money
10 times faster than Warren Buffett, wouldn't she be at the top
of the Forbes 400 list? And if she did have the stock market in the
palm of her hand, why would she want to spend so much time
banging away at her computer keyboard so she could sell $9.99
subscriptions to you?

Let's look at the real numbers, shall we?

Most newsletters are like dragonflies. They look pretty, they
buzz about, but sadly, they don't live very long. In a 12-year study
from June 1980 to December 1992, professors John Graham at the
University of Utah and Campbell Harvey at Duke University tracked
more than 15,000 stock market newsletters. In their findings, 94
percent went out of business sometime between 1980 and 1992.[6]

If you have the Midas touch as a stock picker who spreads pearls
of financial wisdom in a newsletter, you're probably not going to go
out of business. If you can deliver on the promise of high annual
returns, you'll build a newsletter empire. If no one, however, wants
to read what you have to say (because your results are terrible) the
newsletter follows the sad demise of the woolly mammoth.

There are several organizations that track the results of financial newsletter stock picks and *The Hulbert Financial Digest* is one
of them. In its January 2001 edition, the U.S. -based publication
revealed it had followed 160 newsletters that it had considered
solid. But of the 160 newsletters, only 10 of them had beaten the
stock market indexes with their recommendations over the past
decade. Based on that statistic, the odds of beating the stock market indexes by following an investment newsletter are less than
seven percent.[7]

Put another way, how would this advertisement grab you?

You could invest with a total stock market index fund—or
you could follow our newsletter picks. Our odds of failure
(compared with the index) are 93 percent. Sign up now!

If investors knew the truth, financial newsletters probably
wouldn't exist.

High-Yielding Bonds Called "Junk"

At some point, you might fight the temptation to buy a corporate bond paying a high interest percentage. It's probably best to avoid that kind of investment. If a company is financially unhealthy, it's going to have a tough time borrowing money from banks, so it "advertises" a high interest rate to draw riskier investors. But here's the rub: If the business gets into financial trouble, it won't be able to pay that interest. What's worse, you could even lose your initial investment.

Bonds paying high interest rates (because they have shaky financial backing) are called junk bonds.

I've found that being responsibly conservative is better than stretching over a ravine to pluck a pretty flower.

Fast-Growing Markets Can Make Bad Investments

A friend of mine once told me: "My adviser suggested that, because I'm young, I could afford to have all of my money invested in emerging market funds." His financial planner dreamed of the day when billions of previously poor people in China or India would worship their 500-inch, flat-screen televisions, watching *The Biggest Loser* while stuffing their faces with burgers, fries, and gallons of Coke. Eyes sparkle at the prospective burgeoning profits made by investing in fattening economic waistlines. But there are a few things to consider.

Historically, the stock market investment returns of fast-growing economies don't always beat the stock market growth of slow-growing economies. William Bernstein, using data from Morgan Stanley's capital index and the International Monetary Fund, reported in his book, *The Investor's Manifesto*, that fast-growing countries based on gross domestic product (GDP) growth paradoxically have produced lower historical returns than the stock markets in slower growing economies from 1988 to 2008.

Table 8.2 shows that when we take the fastest growing economy (China's economy) and compare it with the slowest growing economy (the U.S.) we see that investors in U.S. stock indexes

Table 8.2 Growing Economies Don't Always Produce Great Stock Market Returns

Country	1988–2008, After Inflation Annualized GDP Growth (in Percentages)	Average Stock Growth (in Percentages)
United States	2.77	8.8
Indonesia	4.78	8.16
Singapore	6.67	7.44
Malaysia	6.52	6.48
Korea	5.59	4.87
Thailand	5.38	4.41
Taiwan	5.39	3.75
China	9.61	−3.31 (as of 1993)

Source: The Investor's Manifesto by William Bernstein

would have made plenty of money from 1993 to 2008. But if investors could have held a Chinese stock market index over the same 15-year period, they would not have made any profits despite China's GDP growth of 9.61 percent a year over that period.

Similarly, as revealed in Table 8.3, Yale University's celebrated institutional investor, David Swensen, warns endowment fund managers not to fall into the GDP growth trap either. In his book written for institutional investors, *Pioneering Portfolio Management*, he suggests from 1985 (the earliest date from which the World Bank's International Finance Corporation began measuring emerging market stock returns) to 2006, the developed countries' stock markets earned higher stock market returns for investors than emerging market stocks did.

Table 8.3 Emerging Market Investors Don't Always Make More Money

Index	1985–2006	$100,000 Invested in Each Index Would Grow to ....
U.S. Index	13.1% annual gain	$1,326,522.75
Developed Stock Market Index (England, France, Canada, Australia)	12.4% annual gain	$1,164,374.09
Emerging Market Index (Brazil, China, Thailand, Malaysia)	12% annual gain	$1,080,384.82

Source: Pioneering Portfolio Management by David Swensen

Emerging markets might be exciting—because they do rise like rockets, crash like meteorites, before rising like rockets again. But if you don't need that kind of excitement in your portfolio, you might be better off going with a total international stock market index fund instead of adding a large emerging-market component.

Whether the emerging markets prove to be future winners is anyone's guess. They might. But it's wise to temper expectations with historical realities, just in case.

Gold Isn't an Investment

Our education systems have done such a lousy job teaching us about money that you can conduct a little experiment out on the streets that I guarantee will deliver shocking results.

Walk up to an educated person and ask them to imagine that one of their forefathers bought $1 worth of gold in 1801. Then ask what they think it would be worth in 2011.

Their eyes might widen at the thought of the great things they could buy today if they sold that gold. They might imagine buying a yacht or Gulfstream jet, or their own island in the South China Sea.

Then break their bubble with the revelation in Figure 8.1. Selling that gold would give them enough money to fill the gas tank of a minivan.

One dollar invested in gold in 1801 would only be worth about $73 by 2011.

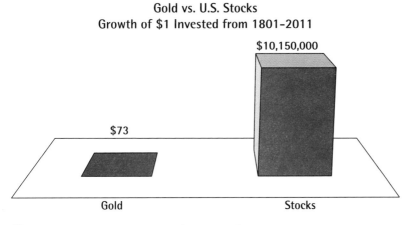

Gold vs. U.S. Stocks
Growth of $1 Invested from 1801–2011

$10,150,000

$73

Gold   Stocks

Figure 8.1   Gold vs. U.S. Stocks (1801–2011)

How about $1 invested in the U.S. stock market?
Now you can start thinking about your yacht.
One dollar invested in the U.S. stock market in 1801 would be worth $10.15 million by 2011.[8]
Gold is for hoarders expecting to trade glittering bars for stale bread after a financial Armageddon. Or it's for people trying to "time" gold's movements by purchasing it on an upward bounce, with the hopes of selling before it drops. That's not investing. It's speculating. Gold has jumped up and down like an excited kid on a pogo stick for more than 200 years, but after inflation, it hasn't gained any long-term elevation.
I prefer the Tropical Beach approach:

1. Buy assets that have proven to run circles around gold (rebalanced stock and bond indexes would do).

2. Lay in a hammock on a tropical beach.

3. Soak in the sun and patiently enjoy the long-term profits.

What You Need to Know about Investment Magazines

If investment magazines were altruistically created to help you achieve wealth, you'd have the same cover story during every issue: Buy Index Funds Today.
But nobody would buy the magazines. It wouldn't be newsworthy. Plus, magazines don't make much money from subscriptions. They make the majority of their money from ads. Pick up a finance magazine and thumb through it to see who's advertising. The financial service industry, selling mutual funds and brokerage services, is the biggest source of advertisement revenue. Few editors would go out on a tree branch to broadcast the futility of picking mutual funds that will beat the market indexes. Advertisers pay the bills for financial magazines. That's why you see magazine covers suggesting: "The Hot Mutual Funds to Buy for 2011."
When I wrote an article in 2005 for *MoneySense* magazine, titled "How I Got Rich on a Middle Class Salary," I mentioned the millionaire mechanic, Russ Perry (who I introduced to you in Chapter 1). I quoted Russ's opinion on buying new cars—that it wasn't a good idea, and that people should buy used cars instead.

Based on a conversation I had with Ian McGugan, the magazine's editor, I learned that one of America's largest automobile manufacturers called McGugan on the phone and threatened to pull its advertisements if it saw anything like that in *MoneySense* again. There are bigger forces at play than those wanting to educate you in the financial magazine industry.

I have an April 2009 issue of *SmartMoney* magazine on my desk as I'm writing this. It would have been written a month earlier when the stock market was reeling from the financial crisis. Instead of shouting out: "Buy stocks now at a great discount!" the magazine was giving people what they wanted: A front cover showing a stack of $100 bills secured by a chain and padlock with the screaming headlines: "Protect Your Money!," "Five Strong Bond Funds," "Where to Put Your Cash," and "How to Buy Gold Now!". Think about it. They have to. If the general public is scared stiff of the stock market's drop, they'll want high doses of chicken soup for their knee-jerking souls. They'll want to know how to escape from the stock market, not embrace it. Giving the public what it pines for when they're scared might sell magazines. But you can't make money being fearful when others are fearful.

I don't mean to pick on *SmartMoney* magazine. I can only imagine the dilemma it faced when putting that issue together. Its writers are smart people. They know—especially for long-term investors—that buying into the stock market when it's on sale is a powerful wealth-building strategy. But a falling stock market, for most people, is scarier than a rectal examination. Touting bond funds and gold was an easier sell for the magazine.

Let's have a look at the kind of money you would have made if you followed that April 2009 edition of *SmartMoney*.

It suggested placing your investment in the following bond funds: the Osterweis Strategic Income Fund <www.osterweis.com/default.asp?P>, the T. Rowe Price Tax-Free Income Fund <www.3troweprice.com/fb2/fbkweb/snapshot.do?ticker=PRTAX>, the Janus High-Yield Fund <https://ww3.janus.com/Janus/Retail/FundDetail?fundID=14>, the Templeton Global Bond Fund <www.franklintempleton.com/retail/app/product/views/fund_page.jsf?fundNumber=406>, and the Dodge & Cox Income Fund <www.dodgeandcox.com/incomefund.asp>.

Table 8.4 shows that with reinvesting the interest, *SmartMoney's* recommended bond funds would have returned an average of 32.8 percent from April 2009 to January 2011.

How about gold, which was also recommended by that edition of *SmartMoney*? Its spectacular run would have seen it gain 46 percent during the same period, as gold was hitting an all-time high.

Table 8.4 Percentages of Growth (April 2009-January 2011)

SmartMoney's Recommended Bond Funds

Osterweis Strategic Income Fund	+34%
T. Rowe Price Tax-Free Income Fund	+13%
Janus High-Yield Fund	+58%
Templeton Global Bond Fund	+34%
Dodge & Cox Income Fund	+25%
Average Return	+32.8%

Source: Morningstar[9]

So far, it looks like the magazine was right on the money, until you look at what they didn't headline. Stock prices were cheaper, relative to business earnings, than they had been in decades. The magazine headlines should have read: "Buy Stocks Now!".

Because they didn't, as demonstrated by Figure 8.2, *Smart-Money* readers missed out on some huge gains, as stocks easily beat bonds and gold from April 2009 to January 2011.

The U.S. stock market (as measured by Vanguard's U.S. stock market index) increased 69 percent, Vanguard's international stock market index rose by 70 percent, and Vanguard's total world index rose by 70 percent during the same period.

The comparative results punctuate how tough predictions can be, while emphasizing that magazines cater for their advertisers and their reader's emotions to sell magazines.

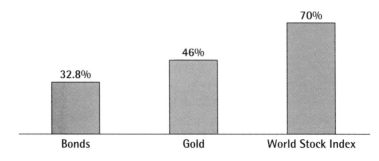

SmartMoney's **Recommendations Fall Short**

Figure 8.2 Bond Funds and Gold vs. Stocks (April 2009-January 2011)
Source: Morningstar[10]

Hedge Funds—The Rich Stealing from the Rich

Some wealthy people turn their noses up at index funds, figuring that if they pay more money for professional financial management, they'll reap higher rewards in the end. Take hedge funds for example. As the investment vehicle for many wealthy, accredited investors (those deemed rich enough to afford taking large financial gambles), hedge funds capture headlines and tickle greed buttons around the world, despite their hefty fees.

But by now, it probably comes as no surprise that, statistically, investing with index funds is a better option. Hedge funds can be risky, and the downside of owning them outweighs the upside.

First the upside

With no regulations to speak of (other than keeping middle-class wage earnings on the sidelines) hedge funds can bet against currencies or bet against the stock market. If the market falls, a hedge fund could potentially make plenty of money if the fund manager "shorts" the market, by placing bets that the markets will fall and then collecting on these bets if the markets crash. With the gift of having accredited (supposedly sophisticated) investors only, hedge fund managers can choose to invest heavily in a few individual stocks—or any other investment product, for that matter—while a regular mutual fund has regulatory guidelines with a maximum number of eggs they're allowed to put into any one basket. If a hedge fund manager's big bets pay off, investors reap the rewards.

Now for the downside

The typical hedge fund charges two percent of the investors' assets annually as an expense ratio, which is one-third more expensive than the expense ratio of the average U.S. mutual fund. Then the hedge funds' management takes 20 percent of their investors' profits as an additional fee to generate profits for fund managers or for the business offering the fund. It's a license to print money off the backs of those hoping for high rewards.

Hedge funds *voluntarily* report their results, which is the first phase of mist over the industry. *The Economist* reports the average (unaudited) returns of hedge funds on the back of each issue, comparing the results to various world indexes. I have been scanning the results for a decade or more, and generally the hedge funds compare favorably—from what I have seen—by a consistent percentage or two above the indexes.

But hedge fund data collectors don't crunch the numbers for the hedge funds that go out of business. They only report the results of those that remain. So what's the attrition rate for these investment products?

When Princeton University's Burton Malkiel and Yale School of Management's Robert Ibbotson conducted an eight-year study of hedge funds from 1996 to 2004, they reported that fewer than 25 percent of funds lasted the full eight years.[11] Would you want to pick from a group of funds with a 75 percent mortality rate? I wouldn't.

When looking at reported average hedge fund returns, you only see the results of the surviving funds—the constantly dying funds aren't factored into the averaging. It's a bit like a coach entering 20 high school kids in a district championship cross-country race. Seventeen drop out before they finish, but your three remaining runners take the top three spots and you report in the school newspaper that your average runner finished second. Bizarre? Of course, but in the fantasy world of hedge fund data crunchers, it's still "accurate."

As a result of such twilight-zone reporting, Malkiel and Ibbotson found during their study that the average returns reported in databases, were overstated by 7.3 percent annually.

These results include survivorship bias (not counting those funds that don't finish the race) and something called "back-fill bias." Imagine 1,000 little hedge funds that are just starting out. As soon as they "open shop" they start selling to accredited investors. But they aren't big enough or successful enough to add their performance figures to the hedge fund data crunchers—yet.

After 10 years, assume that 75 percent of them go out of business, which is in line with Malkiel and Ibbotson's findings. For them, the dream is gone. And it's really gone for the people who invested with them.

Of those (the 250) that remain, half have results of which they're proud, allowing them to grow and to boast of their successful track records. So out of 1,000 new hedge funds, 250 remain after 10 years, and 125 of them grow large enough (based on marketing and success) to report their 10-year historical gains to the data crunchers compiling hedge fund returns. The substandard or bankrupt funds don't get number crunched. Ignoring the weaker funds and highlighting only the strongest ones is called a "backfill bias."

Doing so ignores the mortality of the dead funds and it ignores the funds that weren't successfully able to grow large enough for database recognition. Malkiel and Ibbotson's study found that this bizarre selectiveness spuriously inflated hedge fund returns by 7.3 percent annually over the period of their study. [12]

To make matters even worse, hedge funds are remarkably inefficient after taxes, based on the frequency of their trading. Plus, you never know ahead of time which funds will survive and which funds will die a painful (and costly) death.

Hedge funds are like hedgehogs. Nice to look at from afar, but you really don't want to get too close to their spines. You're far better off in a total stock market index fund.

When investing, seductive promises and get-rich-quicker schemes can be tempting. But they remind me of why I don't take experimental shortcuts when hiking. It's too easy to lose your way. I wonder if the famous French writer, Voltaire, would agree. In a translation from his 1764 *Dictionnaire Philosophique* he wrote: "The best is the enemy of good." [13] Investors who aren't satisfied with a good plan—like indexing—may strive for something they hope will be "best." But that path's wake is filled with more tragedies than successes.

Notes

1. Benjamin Graham (revised by Jason Zweig) *The Intelligent Investor* (New York: Harper Collins Publishers, 2003), 146.
2. Erin Arvedlun, *Madoff, The Man Who Stole $65 Billion* (London: Penguin, 2009), 6.
3. Ibid., 85.
4. "Daryl Joseph Klein and Kleincorp Management Doing Business as Insta-Cash Loans," The Manitoba Securities Commission, order no.5753: August 13, 2008, accessed April 15, 2011, http://www.msc.gov.mb.ca/legal_docs/orders/klein.html.

5. Gilder Technology Report, accessed October 15, 2010, http://www.gildertech.com/.

6. Mel Lindauer, Michael LeBoeuf, and Taylor Larimore, *The Bogleheads Guide to Investing* (Hoboken, New Jersey: John Wiley & Sons, 2007), 158.

7. Ibid., 159.

8. Calculated from 1801–2001 returns of U.S. stocks and gold from Jeremy Siegel, *Stocks for the Long Run,* (New York: McGraw Hill, 2002), then extrapolated further using gold's 2001 price, accessed April 15, 2011, http://www.usagold.com/analysis/2009-gold-prices.html, and compared with its 2011 price, yahoofinance.com.

9. Morningstar.com.

10. Ibid.

11. Swensen, *Pioneering Portfolio Management, An Unconventional Approach to Institutional Investment,* 195.

12. Ibid.

13. Voltaire quote: Famous Quotes, accessed April 15, 2011, http://www.famous-quotes.net/Quote.aspx?The_perfect_is_the_enemy_of_the_good.

RULE 9

The 10% Stock-Picking Solution . . . If You Really Can't Help Yourself

Women might be better investors than men. Various studies around the globe comparing investment account returns for both men and women put women on top.[1] Why is this? Putting women on the household investment podium doesn't make sense to a lot of men. After all, the fairer sex isn't as likely to gather around the water coolers at work, talking up the latest hot stock or mutual fund. They're not as likely to be drooling over CNBC's Becky Quick as she and her co-hosts spout off about stocks, the economy, and the markets on a daily basis. How can women's investment results beat men's results if there are fewer women taking advantage of all the ever-changing information out there?

Finance professors Brad Barber and Terrance Odean suggest that women's investment returns beat men's returns, on average, by roughly one percentage point annually because they trade less frequently, take fewer risks, and expect lower returns, according to a 2009 article by Jason Zweig in *The Wall Street Journal*.[2] Overconfidence, it appears, might be more of a male trait than a female's.

When I've given seminars on indexed investing, many of the women learn to put together a diversified portfolio of indexes. But what has been the greatest risk to their indexed accounts, from what I've seen? Their husbands.

Men more often run the risk of imploding their investment accounts, of chasing get-rich-quick stocks, of trying to second-guess the economy's direction, and of feeling they can take higher risks to gain higher returns.

It sets up the potential for a matrimonial investment war, which might involve the need to compromise. Whether you are a man or a woman, if you really can't refrain from buying individual stocks, then set aside 10 percent of your investment portfolio for stock picking while keeping the remaining 90 percent in a diversified basket of indexes.

When buying individual stocks, do it intelligently. You're not likely to beat the indexes over the long term, but you're sure to have the odd lucky streak, and you might really enjoy the process.

Using Warren Buffett

In 1999, I joined a group of fellow school teachers who pooled some of their money into an investment club. We started out as a rudderless boat. Thinking we were smart, we watched the economic news, subscribed to stock-picking newsletters, followed financial websites, read *The Wall Street Journal* and listened to "experts" on television. And like most people who follow the manic depressive, schizophrenic news of the investment media, our account got hammered.

But then we became Warren Buffett disciples. Unlike the other stock market "gurus" we previously followed, Buffett never claims to know where stock prices are going to go over the short term. Nor does he pontificate about future interest rates or whether a certain company is going to report stronger-than-expected profit earnings that month, quarter, or year.

What he does give us, however, is far more valuable. He teaches how to think clearly and logically about buying businesses at rational prices, suggesting that a business has an intrinsic value and that valuation could always be higher or lower than what the stock market is quoting. In other words, a stock could be worth much more than its current market price. Finding great businesses at fair prices—or better yet, at great prices—is how Buffett has made a fortune in the stock market over time, and our investment club hoped to do the same.

Investment club follows the sage

By the end of 2000, after a rough start, our investment club of school teachers was officially following the Gospel of Warren. We selected stocks based on Buffett-like criteria and we've done well, averaging 8.3 percent annually from October 1999 to January 2011.

In 2004, I began showing our investment holdings and results to Ian McGugan, then editor of *MoneySense*. In 2008, he suggested we "go public" with the story, and I wrote about the club's results and methodology in the November 2008 issue of the magazine.[3]

Since 2008, our club's investments have continued to perform well. But here's the most important part: we don't have any illusions that we will beat the stock market indexes over the long haul. Time has an eroding effect on anyone bold enough to consider beating an index. Loads of smarter investors than us have outperformed the market for a number of years, only to be force-fed a piece of humble pie when they've made a wrong move. Lance Armstrong, the seven-time winner of the Tour De France, wasn't able to keep winning the world's greatest race—as much as he wanted to. And most investors (no matter how they might initially dominate) eventually get spanked by a diversified portfolio of indexes. For that reason, all of my retirement money is tucked away in indexes. That said, if you're still tempted to battle the stock market indexes yourself, let me share what lessons we have learned. Just remember this: no matter what kind of early results you achieve, don't get romanced by the notion that it's going to be easy to beat the market—and don't allocate more than a small portion of your portfolio to individual stocks.

Commit to the Stocks You Buy

I don't believe most millionaires trade stocks. If they own any shares at all, I believe they buy and hold them for long periods, much like they would if they bought a business, an apartment building, or a piece of land. Numerous international studies have shown that, on average, the more you trade, the less you make after taxes and fees.[4] So forget about the high-flying, seductive rants and quacks on CNBC's financial program Squawk Box, convincing you to react to any market hiccup. Forget about fast-paced online newsletter pontifications touting the next hot sector or trading method. Most rich people are committed to their businesses. After all, stocks are businesses, not ticker symbols online. They should be purchased with care and held for years.

Two things you need to have

There are a couple of things that individual stock investors should master. For starters, they need to understand that when stock prices are falling, this is a good thing. Secondly, they need to learn how to identify a great business when they see it.

Hopefully, after reading Chapter 4, you'll have the first part licked. A rising market is a pain in the backside for a long-term investor. If you're going to be buying stock market investments for at least the next five years, you'll prefer to see a stagnating market, or better yet, a falling one. When you've selected a great business, and when the market sends that business into a spiral, you will celebrate and buy more of it. That's what we've done with the investment club. If we choose a solid business, the odds of its eventual recovery are high and short-term market fears let us take advantage of irrational prices.

So How Do You Identify a Great Business?

The first thing you need to know is what you don't know. Bear with me on that paradox. Defining what you don't know can keep you from falling into the black hole of investing. Understanding what a business makes and how much money it generates in sales isn't enough. You need a strong knowledge of how the company works. Obviously, you will never know everything about an individual company. Investors in individual stocks always need to take a leap of faith, but it's much better to understand as much as you can about a business you've elected to buy.

Even when a stock is really popular—such as the current technology favorite Apple <www.apple.com>—if you don't intimately understand the business it's important that you don't buy the stock.

This is the reason our investment club hasn't invested in Apple shares. There's no doubt that it's an amazing business, but we don't know enough about Apple. We don't understand how it plans to keep its competitive advantage. We do know that it was practically a dead company in 2001, and we know that today it's a darling business thanks to trendy, easy-to-use products that have taken the world by storm, but we can't tell you exactly how the business works. We can't tell you what it is developing and why. We can't tell you what big visions it has for its future, and we can't tell you whether those visions will materialize. Most importantly, we can't tell whether it will continue to sell the world's most popular products a decade from now. Maintaining its popularity and technological advantage is imperative to its success. And because we can't gauge how well it can do that in the future, we're not (and probably never will be) qualified to buy Apple stock.

You might be shaking your head as you hear my confession. Perhaps Apple runs within your circle of competence. Perhaps you work in the industry and you have a strong grasp on Apple's products, its future, and its internal finances. If that's the case, then fabulous. You might be fully capable of purchasing and holding Apple as an intelligent investor and business owner. But if you're technologically challenged (like I am) you might want to find more suitable investment waters to wade in.

Simple Businesses Can Ensure More Predictable Profits

The famous U.S. stock picker, Peter Lynch, who led Fidelity's Magellan fund <http://fundresearch.fidelity.com/mutual-funds/summary/316184100> to superb returns in the 1980s, once suggested that you should buy a business that any idiot can run, because one day an idiot will be running it.[5] This is the way it works in business. You won't always have fabulous leaders at the helm of your favorite companies. For that reason, my investment club has always preferred businesses that are simple rather than those that are rapidly changing.

Businesses that change rapidly are complicated, and they're tough for outside investors to analyze. What's more, they're usually more expensive than other businesses. Microsoft's Bill Gates suggests that tech companies should actually be cheaper than old economy businesses, because of their unpredictability. (Old economy refers to older blue-chip industries.) But they aren't. Speaking to business students at the University of Washington in 1998, he said: "I think the [price to earnings] multiples of technology stocks should be quite a bit lower than the multiples of stocks such as Coke and Gillette because we [those running technology companies] are subject to complete changes in the rules."[6]

What will a technology business be doing in the future? Will it be bigger? Smaller? Or will it be extinct?

What's a Price-Earnings Ratio?

A price-earnings ratio (P/E ratio) indicates how cheap or expensive a stock is. The quoted price of a stock, alone, is irrelevant. For example, a $5 stock can be more expensive than a $100 stock.

Here's an example outlined in Table 9.1. Imagine two businesses, each generating $1 million in business profits each year.

Business One is comprised of 5 million shares at $5 each. So if you were to buy the entire company, it would cost $25 million ($5 a share x 5 million shares = $25 million).

If the company's business earnings are $1 million a year and if the price for the entire company is $25 million (at $5 a share), then we know that the price of the company is 25 times greater than the firm's annual earnings.

When a stock trades at a price that's 25 times greater than its annual profits, we can say the stock's P/E ratio is 25.

Imagine Business Two making annual profits of $1 million as well, with shares valued at $100 each on the stock market.

Assume that the business is comprised of 20,000 shares. To buy every share, thereby owning the entire business, would cost $2 million (20,000 shares x $100 per share = $2 million).

Table 9.1   When a $5 Stock Costs More Than a $100 Stock

	Business One	Business Two
Stock price	$5 a share	$100 a share
Annual business profits	$1 million	$1 million
Number of company shares	5 million	20,000
Cost to buy the entire business	$25 million	$2 million
Price of stock relative to business earnings	25X greater	2X greater
Price-to-earnings ratio	25	2

Because the company also generates $1 million in business earnings, we can see that, at $2 million for the entire business, it's trading at two times earnings, for a P/E ratio of two.

Therefore, Business One is far more expensive than Business Two.

When you look at today's technology companies compared with old economy businesses, you can see that the investor in tech stocks takes two types of risks:

1. They're buying businesses with low levels of future predictability.

2. They're buying businesses that are more expensive. See examples in Table 9.2.

You can find tech companies with occasionally lower P/E ratios than older economy companies, but generally people are willing

Table 9.2   Comparative P/E Ratios as of January 2011

P/E Ratios of Tech Stocks	Tech Stocks	P/E Ratios of Old Economy Stocks	Old Economy Stocks
22	Apple (AAPL)	19	Coca-Cola (KO)
23	Oracle (ORCL)	13	Wal-Mart (WMT)
26	Qualcomm (QCOM)	20	General Electric (GE)
22	Agilent Technologies (A)	13	Altria (MO)
25	Google (GOOG)	12	Johnson & Johnson (JNJ)

Source: Yahoo! Finance, price-to-earnings ratios as of January 2011[7]

to pay higher prices for the rush of owning tech stocks —even though, as an aggregate, they tend to produce lower returns than old economy stocks when all dividends are reinvested.

In Jeremy Siegel's enlightening book, *The Future for Investors— Why the Tried and True Beats the Bold and New*, the Wharton business professor concludes an exhaustive search indicating that when investors reinvest their dividends, they're far better off buying old economy stocks than new economy (tech) stocks. Dividend payouts for old economy stocks tend to be higher, so when reinvested, they can automatically purchase a greater number of new shares. New shares automatically purchased with dividends means that there are now more shares to gift further dividends. The effect snowballs. This is the main reason Siegel found that history's most profitable stocks over the past 50 years have names such as Exxon Mobil <www.exxonmobil.com/Corporate>, Johnson & Johnson <www.jnj.com>, and Coca-Cola <www.coca-cola.com>, instead of names such as IBM <www.ibm.com> and Texas Instruments <www.ti.com>.[8]

Most investors don't realize this. They're willing to pay more for the sexiness of high-tech stocks, which is one of the reasons most patient investors in old economy stocks tend to easily beat most tech stock purchasers over the long haul.

Stocks With Staying Power

Because you can't control a business's management decisions, you should pick stocks that are long-standing leaders in their fields.

One of my investment club's best purchases was Coca-Cola in 2004. We had the good fortune to buy it at $39 a share and were confident that we were getting a great business at a fair price. The stock price, however, has risen 72 percent since then, dampening our enthusiasm for additional shares based on a higher P/E ratio. The reason I call it one of our best purchases is because of its durable competitive advantage, coupled with the price we paid and the near inevitability of this company making far greater business profits 20 years from now. We feel confident that we won't have to watch Coca-Cola's business operations every quarter—that the business is nearly certain to generate higher profits 5 years from now, 10 years from now, even 20 years from now. Coca-Cola, after all, has a

Table 9.3   Coca-Cola's Consistent Profit Growth

Three-Year Periods	Average Earnings Per Share
1985–1987	26 cents
1988–1990	43 cents
1991–1993	72 cents
1994–1996	$1.19
1997–1999	$1.45
2000–2002	$1.57
2003–2005	$2.06
2006–2008	$2.65
2009–2010	$3.21

Source: Value Line Investment Survey: Coca Cola[9]

longstanding history of making more and more money. If we take its historical business earnings and divide them into three-year periods, we can see how consistently the company continues to grow. Table 9.3 shows Coca-Cola's earnings per share data since 1985.

Any way you slice it, emerging markets are helping to fuel even higher profits for Coca-Cola. The case volume of sales in India, for example, reported in Coca-Cola's 2010 annual report, reveals a 17 percent increase from the year before, and the Southern Eurasia region reported 20 percent case volume growth in 2010 from a year earlier.[10] Coca-Cola could continue to be one of the world's most predictable businesses in the future, thanks to its wide (and growing) customer base, its myriad of drinks under its label, and its strong competitive position.

That said, there's a lot more to valuing a good business than figuring out if it will still have a competitive advantage years from now.

Buy businesses that increase the price of the products they sell

You've probably already gathered that the investment game is like playing odds. There's only one guarantee: invest in a low-cost index fund and you'll make the return of that market plus its dividends, and you'll beat the vast majority of professional investors over time. It's not foolproof; we have no idea where the markets will be five or ten years from now. Still, it's the closest thing we have to a stock market guarantee.

Picking individual stocks is a lot more treacherous. So how do you put the odds of success in your favor?

Buy businesses that are relatively easy to run and make sure the price of those business products are going to rise with inflation. An example of a business that *doesn't* meet those criteria is U.S. computer maker Dell. It's a fabulous company, but it's cursed by falling prices for its computer products. Most technology companies, after all, end up selling their products at lower prices over time. Think about how much it cost for your first laptop computer and how much cheaper (and better) laptops are today. It's getting cheaper for companies such as Dell to make their computers (which is one reason for their lower product prices), but lowering product prices can put a strain on profit margins. In other words, when Dell sells a $1,000 computer, after taxes and manufacturing-related costs, how much money does Dell pocket? From 2001 to 2005, Dell's average net profit margin was 6.34 percent. The company reaped an average of $63.40 for every $1,000 sold. And from 2006 to 2010, Dell's average profit margin was 4.08 percent—providing just $40.80 for every $1,000 of products that were sold.[11]

Lowering product prices threatens the company's long-term profitability, making it tough for the business to record the same kind of future profits without continually pushing itself to create something better every year (a concern PepsiCo and Coca-Cola don't need to worry about as much). If you put yourself in a cryogenic chamber and woke up 20 years from now, would Dell be a household computer name? It could be, or then again, it might bite the dust like so many tech companies before it.

In contrast, businesses such as Coca-Cola, Johnson & Johnson, and PepsiCo <www.pepsico.com> are far more likely to be market leaders in 20 years. Unlike technology-based businesses, these companies increase the prices of the products they sell partly because of consumer loyalty for their brands. They don't have as much pressure to keep coming up with "the next great product" unlike most technology-based businesses. They can create a product, market it, and expect people to enjoy it many years into the future. That's not the case with tech companies, which eventually have to slash the prices of their products to attract buyers who may otherwise be attracted to a competitor's newly introduced tech gadget, creating a much tougher (and arguably more competitive) business environment.

Learn to love low-debt levels

History is full of periods of economic duress—as well as economic prosperity. And the future will have its fair share of each.

Many professional stock pickers like businesses with low debt because they can weather economic storms more effectively. It makes sense. If fewer people are buying a company's product due to an economic recession, then the high-debt business is going to suffer. Money they've borrowed will still saddle them with interest payments, and they will likely be forced to lay off employees or sell assets (manufacturing equipment, buildings, and land) to meet those payments. Even if they have a fairly durable competitive advantage in their field, if they have to sell off too many assets, they probably won't maintain that advantageous position for long.

An example of a business without debt, which our investment club purchased in 2005, is Fastenal <www.fastenal.com>. The company sells building-supply materials and has successfully expanded its operation throughout the U.S. and beyond. But business slowed when a recession hit the U.S. in 2008, hammering the home-construction industry. Not having long-term debt, however, ensured it didn't have to meet the bank's loan requirements. If anything, the recession could end up being a good thing for a disciplined, debt-free or low-debt business. Such a company could acquire the assets of struggling businesses, making them even stronger when the recession ends.

You can see that investors have treated Fastenal's debt-free balance sheet with plenty of respect as well. During a slowdown for building-material suppliers, Fastenal's shares in late 2010 should have been priced a lot lower than they were five years ago when the U.S. housing market was in its full-bubbled boom.

But Fastenal's shares haven't struggled nearly as much as the company's counterparts. Figure 9.1 reveals that (as of January 2011) they were priced higher than they were five years previous at the height of the building boom.

Some investors like to look at businesses' debt-to-equity ratio. In others words, how much debt does a company have relative to assets? That's fair enough. But I've always preferred choosing businesses (preferably) with no debt at all.

It's especially wise to give ourselves a margin of safety when it comes to company debt. Some people refer to "good debt" and

Figure 9.1   Fastenal's Debt-Free Balance Sheet Gives Price Stability During Recession
Source: Yahoo! Finance[12]

"bad debt." In the case of "good debt," many figure that if a business can borrow money at eight percent, then make 15 percent on that borrowed money (within the business) then gain a tax credit on the loan's interest, it will come out ahead. The logic is sound. But if a company's revenue dries up during a recession, then the eight percent loan can loom over the company like the grim reaper.

But how much debt is too much? That probably depends on the business.

The debt-to-equity ratio has its limitations. In theory, the lower the debt is relative to assets (equity), the better. But I generally set a standard for my investments that doesn't involve a debt-to-equity comparison. After all, if a business has equity in manufacturing equipment, why would I want it selling its equipment to pay bank loans during tough times? That just shoots the money machine in the foot. The company needs its machinery (and its other assets) to generate revenue in most cases, so I wouldn't want it selling the very things it needs to create future sales. As a result, I ignore the comparison between debt and equity, preferring to see the company's debt-to-earnings comparisons instead.

For me, if the firm's annual net income (when averaging the previous three year's earnings) is higher than or very close to

Business	Stock Ticker Symbol	Average Annual Net Income From 2007 to 2009	2010 Long-Term Debt	Time to Pay Off Long-Term Debt, Based on Average Annual Earnings
COCA-COLA (Soft drinks)	KO	$6.657 billion	$5 billion	Roughly 9 months
JOHNSON & JOHNSON (Pharmaceutical, medical devices, consumer products)	JNJ	$12.646 billion	$7.9 billion	Roughly 7 months
MICROSOFT (Software)	MSFT	$15.438 billion	$4.939 billion	Roughly 4 months
EXXON MOBIL (Oil)	XOM	$35 billion	$17 billion	Roughly 6 months
STARBUCKS (Coffee shops, retail coffee)	SBUX	$512 million	No debt	No debt
ABERCROMBIE & FITCH (Clothing retail)	ANF	$249 million	$75 million	Roughly 3–4 months
STRYKER (Medical devices)	SYK	$1.02 billion	$1.08 billion	Roughly 12 months

Figure 9.2 Sample of Businesses With Low Debt, Relative to Income
Source: Value Line Investment Survey[13]

the company's debt level, then the company is conservatively financed enough for my tastes.

Figure 9.2 lists a few well-known, global companies that fit my "conservatively financed" requirement.

Efficient businesses make dollars and sense

Think about this one from a logical business perspective. Imagine having the choice between buying two businesses that each generated net income averaging $1 billion over the past three years.

Assume that they're both growing their earnings at the same rate, and assume that they each have the same level of debt. They're also both in industries where the goods will likely be used for many years to come and each business can increase the price of its products with inflation. But there's a difference:

Business A generates its $1 billion profits off $10 billion in plants/machinery and other assets.

Business B generates its $1 billion profits off $5 billion in plants/machinery and other assets.

Which business are you going to be more comfortable with?

My answer would be Company B because it's more efficient. If it can generate $1 billion from $5 billion in assets/materials, then it has a return on total capital of 20 percent ($1 billion divided by $5 billion = 0.20)

Company A has a return on total capital of 10 percent because it generates profits that are only one-tenth the value of its assets. ($1 billion divided by $10 billion = 0.10)

Return on total capital measures how efficiently a business uses both shareholders' capital and debt to produce income. I believe the value of a company ultimately rests on its proven historical ability to earn a significant and reliable profit on the money that's invested in its business.

I recommend that any serious stock picker should order a subscription through investment-research provider Value Line, which gives you access to thousands of businesses around the world. And you can use its portfolio screens to figure out which companies have the highest rates of return on total capital and then narrow those down to see which businesses have been able to earn those returns consistently.

Looking for businesses with a high single year's return on total capital means little. If a company has a single great year, or if they're creative with their accounting, they could post a high return on capital that won't necessarily be sustainable as it goes forward. You want to look for durable businesses with long histories of efficiency.

As of October 2010, when I analyzed more than 2,000 businesses in the Value Line investment survey, fewer than 10 percent of them had returns on total capital exceeding 15 percent.

Refining the search further to find the percentage of businesses with a 10-year track record averaging 15 percent on total capital, I found only five percent of the 2,000-plus businesses fit the bill, including TJX Companies <www.tjx.com>, Weight Watchers <www.weightwatchers.com>, Garmin <www.garmin.com>, Colgate Palmolive <www.colgate.com>, Coach <www.coach.com>, Stryker <www.stryker.com>, Heinz <www.heinz.com>, Microsoft <www.microsoft.com>, Coca-Cola <www.coca-cola.com>, PepsiCo

<www.pepsico.com>, Johnson & Johnson <www.jnj.com>, and Starbucks <www.starbucks.com>. By using Value Line's stock screen, you can find nearly 100 other businesses with 10-year track records that have averaged 15 percent or more on their total capital.

Demand honesty

Besides finding economically efficient businesses, it's also important for investors to seek businesses with honest managers. Executives should strive to be candid with shareholders and they should always think of enriching shareholders first, themselves second.

The most reliable way to find such management is to look for firms with a high level of insider ownership by top executives. If managers are shareholders themselves—especially if they own 10 percent or more of the stock—they're more likely to take shareholders' interests to heart.

You might think firms would have to be relatively small for insiders to own a high percentage of the shares, but that's not necessarily the case. Companies with more than 20 percent insider ownership include Netflix <www.netflix.com>, Papa John's International <www.ir.papajohns.com>, Nu Skin Enterprises <www.nuskin.com>, Berkshire Hathaway <www.berkshirehathaway.com>, Estee Lauder <www.esteelauder.com>, and the publisher of this book, John Wiley & Sons <www.wiley.com>, to name just a few.

If you really like a business, but it doesn't have a high percentage of insider ownership, you can look for other factors indicating the company puts shareholder interests first. One such factor is executive pay.

It's easy to find out online how much executives of publically traded companies get paid. Compare the company you're interested in with a few other businesses in the same industry. If the businesses make roughly the same amount of money, and the industry is the same, then their pay should be comparable. But if one chief executive officer's pay isn't in line with the others (by a wide margin), then you might have found a company that isn't putting its shareholder interests first.

Huge paychecks are just one symptom of questionable management. I also dislike companies that play games with their earnings to satisfy analysts. A prime example is the way some companies buy back shares. Doing so can make sense if management believes the shares are undervalued, therefore representing a good use of company money. But some companies turn this policy on its head, selling shares to raise money when the share price is cheap, then turning around and buying back shares when the markets are hot and shares are trading at ultra-expensive levels of 30 or 40 times their earnings. This insane ritual burns through a company's cash—essentially it consists of buying high and selling low—and the only motivation is the management's desire to fine-tune its earnings per share to satisfy the expectations of security analysts. Such games are maddening. They destroy shareholders' wealth.

Scuttlebutt like a detective

I've become a really big fan of online stock screens (such as Value Line) for narrowing down lists of businesses that meet selected, customized financial criteria, but for serious investors, stock screens are a starting point, not an ending point. The late Philip Fisher, author of *Common Stocks and Uncommon Profits*, devised a pre-Internet system of kicking the tires of companies that interested him by visiting the customers of the businesses he liked while questioning their competitors as well. He would ask great questions like: "What are the strengths and weaknesses of your competitors?" and "What should you be doing (but are not yet doing) to maintain your competitive advantage?"[14]

The key isn't to walk into a company's public relations department and ask these questions. It's to get in on the ground floor, where the products are being created, sold, or distributed, and ask there. The Internet can be a great source of information, but it can make people lazy, tempting us to skip getting a "hands-on" feel for our businesses.

When I see a residential construction site, for example, I often wander in and ask them what fastening construction brackets they're using. Simpson Manufacturing <www.simpsonmfg.com> is a business that my investment club owns shares in, and I'm always curious to see who's using the products, what they like about them, and what they dislike about them. If I wander onto construction sites and hear Simpson, Simpson, Simpson, and how easy the representatives are to work with, and how great the products are,

then I've established ground-floor information that I might not necessarily find on the Internet.

As a business owner, I think it's very important to know your
company well. Don't experiment with shortcuts; you could end up
getting lost.

Set your price

Once you've decided which stocks look good, you have to get
them at the right price. But what is a good price? Again, think of
yourself as a business owner buying an entire company.

Let's take Starbucks as an example. As of this writing, it trades
at $26 a share and there are 740 million shares in the company.
That makes the entire business worth roughly $19.2 billion.

Over the past three years, its net income has averaged $598
million after posting profits of $672 million in 2007, $525 million
in 2008, and $598 million in 2009.

If we owned the entire company, and if we paid $19.2 billion for
it, we would want to know what our return on investment would
be, annually, if we averaged $598 million a year in net profits.

When dividing $598 million by $19.2 billion, we get a return
(also known as an earnings yield) of 3.1 percent.

It makes sense when thinking of it from a business sense. If you
bought the entire business for $19.2 billion, and if you made $598 million after all expenses and taxes, you would have made 3.1 percent
on your $19.2 billion.

Is that a good deal? It depends on the alternatives. You can start
by comparing the yield from your stock with the yield on a 10-year
government bond. No stock is as safe as government bonds since
governments—at least those in highly developed countries —don't go
bust. You would therefore be silly to take on the risk involved in buying a stock if it yields less than a risk-free bond. In fact, since future
earnings on any stock are uncertain, you should make sure any shares
you buy yield a bit more than the 10-year bond. The extra yield com-
pensates you for the risk you're embracing in buying the stock.

How much yield you should demand is a matter of judgment.
If a company has been growing rapidly, you may be willing to buy
its stock when the average of earnings from the past three years
works out to slightly more than the equivalent of a 10-year bond

yield. On the other hand, if a firm is growing slowly, you might not want to buy its stock until you feel satisfied that it will provide you with at least a tenth more in earnings than a 10-year government bond. So if the bond were yielding, say, five percent, you would demand at least a 5.5 percent yield from the stock before you would be willing to purchase it.

Halfway through 2010, our club bought shares in the internationally ubiquitous company, Johnson & Johnson, at $57 a share. Over the past three years, its net income had averaged $12.64 billion, and when multiplying that by the number of shares in existence, you can calculate what it would cost to buy the entire company: roughly $160 billion. Dividing the average three-year net income ($12.64 billion) by the cost of the total company ($160 billion) gives us an annual earnings yield of 7.9 percent.[15]

When comparing that yield with a yield of a 10-year U.S. government bond (which paid 2.52 percent) I realized we were being well compensated for the added risk of owning the stock instead of a bond, so we bought shares in the company.

Selling Stocks

I think stockowners should hold their companies for long periods, but there are instances when it's wise to sell:

1. If the company deviated from its core business.

2. If the stock was grossly overpriced.

The first reason for selling is self-explanatory. If a company's ability to make chocolate is legendary, but it decided to switch gears to pursue space tourism (something it has no track record in) then it might be wise to bail on the shares.

The second reason to sell requires some judgment and a bit of math.

When we sold Schering Plough

Schering Plough (which can no longer be purchased on the stock market, since Merck <www.merck.com> purchased it in 2009) met

Table 9.4   Schering Plough's Earnings per Share

Year	Schering Plough's Earnings per Share
2001	$1.58
2002	$1.34
2003	$0.31

Source: Value Line Investment Survey–Schering Plough 2005 Report[16]

my investment club's purchase requirements in 2003, and we paid $15.24 a share. Its blockbuster allergy medication, Claritin, was losing its patent protection, allowing other companies to be able to sell a generic version for a fraction of the cost. This was one of the reasons Schering Plough's price was hammered from about $40 a share in 2002 down to slightly more than $15 a share in 2003. I felt that Wall Street's reaction to the Claritin patent was overdone and highly emotional.

Prior to the price drop, despite being a great business, Schering Plough hadn't interested me. Buying the stock at $40 a share would have been taking a huge risk because the earnings yield would have been just 3.8 percent. This was less than what a government bond was paying at the time, and there was the added risk of the looming Claritin patent expiration. Despite that risk, I certainly didn't expect Wall Street to hammer the stock all the way down to $15.

While we weren't attracted to Schering Plough at $40 a share (with an earning yield of 3.8 percent) we were much more interested when the earnings yield more than doubled.

The earnings levels for Schering Plough in the three years before we purchased shares can be seen in Table 9.4.

The average earnings for the previous three years represented $0.75 a share. At $15.24, that represented an earning's yield of seven percent. We bought our first shares and hoped, of course, the price would fall further.

By 2008, however, Schering Plough's price had risen to $25 a share, and the earnings yield based on the previous three years—2005, 2006, and 2007—gave the business an earnings yield of just three percent annually. This was below the interest yield on a 10-year government bond (which paid roughly four percent at the time) so we sold the shares at $25.[17]

A 64 percent profit over three years might sound impressive, but you also could view it as a disappointment. Investing is a lot easier if the businesses you buy (at good prices) grow at a pace relative to their earnings growth. Then, if the business doesn't deviate from its business model and if most of the reasons you bought the business in the first place still apply, you can keep holding the shares as they grow, long term, while earning healthy dividends along the way.

As I mentioned before, we rarely sell individual stocks, and to be honest, many of the stocks we have sold eventually went on to new highs without us. You could count Schering Plough as an example—Merck bought them out for $28 a share (12 percent higher than the company's stock price when we sold our shares).

Generally, the fewer trades you make in your investment account, the more money you'll make. Whether you're a mutual fund manager or a personal stock picker, lower trades equate to lower costs and taxes—and generally higher returns.

Committing to stocks for a long period of time, however, requires that you know as much about your companies as possible. To ensure the highest odds of familiarity, you may want to choose simple, predictable businesses, while opting for those that are efficiently run and likely to stand the test of time. Also consider what a financial tsunami could do to your businesses. Low-debt levels can be solid foundations—especially during tough times.

When you have found a business that you want to buy, analyze its price as if you were buying the entire business. The return you make can be highly dependent on the price you pay. But even with the best stock-picking tools, the odds are high that eventually most stock pickers will lose to market-tracking indexes, especially after factoring in transaction costs and taxes. It's fun to fight the tide. But you should invest the bulk of your money intelligently with a diversified account of indexes.

Notes

1. "Women Better Investors Than Men," BBC News online, accessed April 16, 2011, http://news.bbc.co.uk/2/hi/business/4606631.stm.
2. Jason Zweig, "How Women Invest Differently Than Men," *The Wall Street Journal*, May 12, 2009, accessed April 16, 2011, http://finance.yahoo.com/focus-retirement/article/107064/How-

Women-Invest-Differently-Than-Men?mod=fidelity-building-wealth.

3. Andrew Hallam, "How We Beat the Market," *MoneySense*, November 2008, 44–48.

4. Paul Farrell, "Day-Traders Lose Big, Still Live in Denial: 77 percent of American Traders are 'Losers' While 82 percent of Day-Traders in Taiwan-China Are Bigger 'Losers,'" *Wall Street Warzone*, June 16, 2010, accessed November 13, 2010, http://wallstreetwarzone.com/the-more-you-trade-the-less-you-earn/.

5. "The Greatest Investors: Peter Lynch," Investopedia, accessed November 13, 2010, http://www.investopedia.com/university/greatest/peterlynch.asp.

6. Timothy Vick, *How To Pick Stocks Like Warren Buffett* (New York: McGraw-Hill, 2001), 170–171.

7. Yahoo! Finance: Price to earnings ratios as of January 2011.

8. Jeremy Siegel, *The Future For Investors, Why The Tried And True Triumph Over The Bold and New* (New York: Random House, 2005), 7–9.

9. Value Line Investment Survey: Coca-Cola, January 28, 2011, accessed April 16, 2011, http://www3.valueline.com/dow30/f2084.pdf.

10. The Coca-Cola Company 2010 Annual Report, (http://www.the-coca-colacompany.com/investors/pdfs/form_10K_2010.pdf) 57.

11. Value Line Investment Survey: Dell, April 8, 2011.

12. Fastenal, historical price source, Yahoo! Finance, accessed April 16, 2011, http://finance.yahoo.com/q/hp?s=FAST&a=09&b=1&c=2005&d=09&e=17&f=2010&g=d.

13. The Value Line Investment Survey: 2011 reports for Coca-Cola, Johnson & Johnson, Microsoft, Exxon Mobil, Starbucks, Abercrombie & Fitch, and Stryker.

14. Philip A. Fisher, *Common Stocks and Uncommon Profits and Other Writings* (Hoboken, New Jersey: John Wiley & Sons, 2003), 45.

15. Value Line Investment Survey: Johnson & Johnson, accessed April 16, 2011, http://www3.valueline.com/dow30/f4979.pdf.

16. Value Line Investment Survey: Schering Plough, 2008 Report.

17. Ibid.

The Nine Rules of Wealth Checklist

You probably know a few people who are financial train wrecks waiting to happen. You, however, have a choice. You can pass them by as they smash themselves up, or you can teach them a few strategies to empower them to make good financial decisions. This isn't taught in schools, so most people spend far too much money on material things, invest inefficiently, and allow fear and greed to manipulate their wealth levels.

With luck, one day many of the principles outlined in this book will become part of a mandatory high school curriculum. Doing so would go a long way to ensure that people invest responsibly, which in turn will force the financial service industry to limit its gouging of individual investors.

No matter what your age and current level of wealth, you can build financial security by using the nine rules outlined in this book:

1. Spend like a millionaire (or less) if you want to become rich.

2. Start investing as early as possible—after paying off credit card debt and any other high-interest loans.

3. Invest in low-cost index funds instead of actively managed funds. Nobody can consistently pick "winning" actively managed funds ahead of time.

4. Understand stock market history and psychology so you don't fall victim to the craziness that infects every investing generation (often more than once).

5. Learn to build a complete, balanced portfolio with stock and bond index funds that will easily beat most of the pros.

6. Create indexed accounts no matter where you live.

7. Learn to fight an adviser's sales rhetoric.

8. Avoid investment schemes and scams that tickle your greed button.

9. If you must buy common stocks, do it with a small percentage of your portfolio and pick a mentor such as Warren Buffett.

Live long, prosper, and pass on what you have learned.

Index